Creating Unicorns with Simple Innovations: The PISA Method

Creating Unicorns with Simple Innovations: The PISA Method

Jorge Sá
Magda Pereira
Nadiia Nikitina

BEP
BUSINESS EXPERT PRESS
Leader in applied, concise business books

Creating Unicorns with Simple Innovations: The PISA Method

Cover design by Vasconcellos e Sá Associates

Interior design by S4Carlisle Publishing Services, Chennai, India

First published in 2025 by
Business Expert Press, LLC
222 East 46th Street, New York, NY 10017
www.businessexpertpress.com

ISBN-13: 978-1-63742-827-6 (paperback)
ISBN-13: 978-1-63742-828-3 (e-book)

Business Expert Press Entrepreneurship and Small Business Management Collection

First edition: 2025

10 9 8 7 6 5 4 3 2 1

EU SAFETY REPRESENTATIVE
Mare Nostrum Group B.V.
Mauritskade 21D
1091 GC Amsterdam
The Netherlands
gpsr@mare-nostrum.co.uk

Dedication

*This book is dedicated to
all **entrepreneurs** who created
unicorns through **simplicity**.*

Acknowledgments

This book would not have been possible without the continuous support and highly valuable improvements made by many, including the managing editor Scott Isenberg, Professor Scott Shane, Charlene Kronstedt, and Nandini Loganathan, among others.

To all our gratitude. Naturally that any shortcomings are the sole responsibility of the authors.

Description

The Untold Story

Elon Musk, Steve Jobs, Bill Gates, Mark Zuckerberg, Michael Dell, Pierre Omidyar, and so many others are **technical genius**. Glamorous.

But their glamour obscures the reality of **another type** of genius, which, **today**, has an equally great impact on people's lives. Rather than with technical sophistication they create great value through **simplicity**. And in return, the market makes **unicorns** (companies valued at $1 billion or more) out of them.

Examples are: Spanx, Rent the Runway, Dollar Shave Club, Gorillas, Warby Parker, GymShark, Fenty Beauty, Harry's, Vestiaire Collective, Gousto, or Havaianas, to name just a few.

And there are many other **simple** innovations that, although not yet achieving unicorn status, are nevertheless of **high value**, in the multitude of millions: Knix, Readerest, Bizchair.com, Drop Stop, Lisa Gable Accessories, Pouchee, Eyelights, TRX, Chawel, and so on.

In the past when life was plainer and its pace smoother, simplicity was not so much valued. Today it is the source of innumerous successes. **Simplicity** is complexity solved and thus the greatest sophistication.

Besides **technology**, simplicity is today a *second venue* for successful entrepreneurship.

However, although simple innovations are more accessible to all, regardless of their age, background, and education, that does not mean they are **easy**, as in life, what is simple is to complicate and what is complicated is to simplify.

Thus, there is a need for a **method to create simple innovations**, which are the *great second venue* for entrepreneurship. That is what the **PISA method** does with its five basic characteristics:

1st: Extremely **valuable** and technologically **simple** innovations;

2nd: The opportunities **came** to the entrepreneurs (instead of they having actively to **look for** them);

3rd: **Tests:** two types and only two are worthwhile; to rely on people's **emotions** and **actions** (not on their **thoughts** and **words**);

4th: The **solutions** already exist elsewhere (instead of having to be **created** from scratch); and finally

5th: **Action** (implementation) can be nonexpensive while minimizing risk.

Although each entrepreneur has a specific story and they vary in many characteristics from age to background and despite having no special know-how, across all of them there are some **repeated** themes that represent **common** links. That is the essence of the **PISA method**, which summarizes the actions of visionaries who touched lives by simplifying an increasingly complex world.

And so in a certain sense this book was written by the multitude of entrepreneurs whose lives are nothing but examples of the PISA method, detailing a quiet revolution underway, which falls below the radar and therefore has, so far, been an **untold story**.

Contents

CHAPTER 1

Unicorns Through Simple Innovations: Overview of the PISA Method

The key to great innovations is not to try to be brilliant but to be simple.

Peter Drucker
(founder of modern management)

1.1. The Untold Story

Elon Musk, Steve Jobs, Bill Gates, Mark Zuckerberg, Michael Dell, Pierre Omidyar, and so many others are **technical genius**. Hard to be taught.

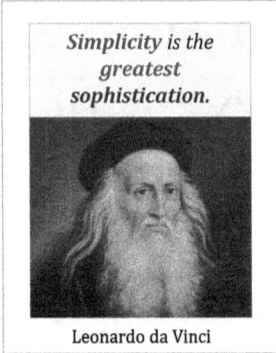

Simplicity is the greatest sophistication.

Leonardo da Vinci

But their glamour obscures the reality of **another type** of genius, which has an equally great impact on people's lives. Rather than with technical sophistication they create great value through **simplicity**. And in return, the market makes **unicorns**[1] out of them.

The next chapters will share many examples: Spanx, Rent the Runway, Dollar Shave Club, Gorillas, Warby Parker, GymShark, Fenty Beauty, Harry's, Vestiaire Collective, or Gousto, to name just a few.

And many other simple innovations although not yet achieving unicorn status are nevertheless of high value in the hundreds of millions: Knix, Readerest, Bizchair.com, Drop Stop, Lisa Gable Accessories, Pouchee, Eyelights, TRX, and so on.

Their genius lies in touching the lives of millions with **simplicity**, which, as said, is complexity solved and thus the greatest sophistication.

In the past when life was plainer and its pace smoother, simplicity was not so much valued. Today it is the source of innumerous successes.

Spanx? Became a unicorn in less than two decades. And what is basically Spanx?

---

[1] Companies valued at $1 billion or more.

In the words of founder Sara Blakely (who previously, among other failures, flunked the admission exam for Florida State Law School and did not succeed as a stand-up comedian) *simply footless body shaping pantyhoses*.

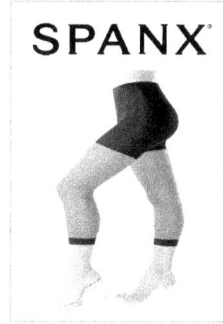

Why footless? Because she cut short (by legs length) the standard pantyhoses, making them less warm and the foot seams not visible when wearing sandals or open shoes. That was the original product.[2]

Rent the Runway took half the time of Spanx to become a unicorn, only a decade, and was the product of Jenn Hyman seeing her sister flirting with credit card debt to buy new dresses for weddings.

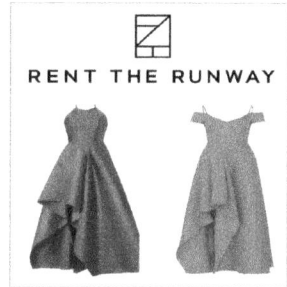

The solution? An e-commerce platform *to rent designer apparel*.

Then *Dollar Shave Club* cut again the time to become a unicorn in half: only five years—by being a home delivery of razors and blades and later adding other grooming products: creams, lotions, and so on, and thus offering convenience and low price.

And *Gorillas*, a home delivery grocery company with a 10-minute guarantee, became a unicorn in … nine months.

So, the point in **Figure 1** is straightforward: *unicorns do not have to be technically complex*. They can and indeed are frequently quite **simple**.

---

[2]With time the company expanded its product portfolio: footless body shaping pantyhoses half leg, below knee, above ankle, bras, leggings, and so on.

Company name	Initial product	Time to unicorn
Spanx	Footless body shaping pantyhoses	Two decades
Rent the Runway	E-commerce platform to rent designer dresses	One decade
Dollar Shave Club	Home delivery of razors	Five years
Gorillas	10-minute delivery of grocery products	Nine months
Warby Parker	Home delivery of designer glasses	Five years
GymShark	Nonexpensive designer gym wear	Eight years
Fenty Beauty	All-inclusive makeup products for all skin tones and types	One year
Harry's	Home delivery of grooming products	Six years
Vestiaire Collective	Online platform to trade high fashion clothes	Two decades
Gousto	Meal kit boxes delivered to consumers' doorsteps	Eight years

Figure 1 A few examples of simple unicorns

Thus, **simplicity** is, besides **technology**, a *second venue* for successful entrepreneurship.

However, although simple innovations are more accessible, that does not mean they are easy. In life, what is simple is to complicate and what is complicated is to simplify.

Thus, there is a need for a **method to create simple innovations**, which are the *great second venue* for entrepreneurship. That is what the **PISA method** is about.

Naturally each entrepreneur in Figure 1 has his/her[3] specific story. But across all of them there are some repeated themes that represent **common** links.

---

[3]Henceforth whenever written she or his should be equally read he or her. The same applies to men or women. All types. All genres. Whatever.

Looking from afar they are more noticeable, easier to identify, and can thus through induction be (1) schematized, (2) put in proper order, and (3) presented as a sequence of steps to allow to replicate great innovations benefiting from the experience of others.

And sure enough there are examples of entrepreneurs who just stumbled into great innovations. They were lucky. The stories of chocolate chip cookies, Coca-Cola, or Levi's are examples.

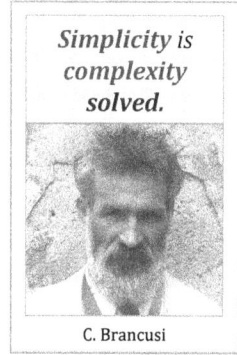

Simplicity is complexity solved.

C. Brancusi

But why **wait** for luck to come to us when we can **create** our own luck?

Why to fumble and grope at our own cost instead of standing on others' shoulders to shortcut market success?

So in a certain sense this book was written by the multitude of entrepreneurs whose lives are nothing but examples of the PISA method with **its five basic characteristics**:

1st: Extremely **valuable** and technologically **simple** innovations;
2nd: The opportunities **came** to the entrepreneurs (instead of they having actively to **look for** them);
3rd: **Tests**: two types and only two are worthwhile; to rely on people's **emotions** and **actions** (not on their **thoughts** and **words**);
4th: The **solutions** already exist elsewhere (instead of having to be **created** from scratch); and finally
5th: **Action** (implementation) can be nonexpensive while minimizing risk.

That is the essence of the **PISA method**, which summarizes the actions of visionaries who touched lives by simplifying an increasingly complex world.

1.2. Overview of the PISA method:
Problem–Inquire–Solve–Action

Cooltan
Tan Through Shirts & Swimwear

BAGTAG

The next chapters will detail the basic steps of the PISA method, which starts by seeing entrepreneurs as **problem solvers**.

Men and women who tackle opportunities disguised as problems. Of **five** types:

First **bothers**, more than simple inconveniences almost aggravations, whose solution constitutes thus great opportunities, such as Cooltan, Funktional, Pencil Bugs, Bagtag.[4]

Then daily life brings a second type of opportunities: **incompetent products**, goods that when used lack one extra quality and consequently are not quite up to the task. They come out short. Examples are Elevators, The Sleep Styler, Drop Stop, or Soundbender.

Third are **complications**, to be erased by flexible, versatile products, further simplifying our lives: Day2Night, Tanya Heath, Chawel, Pouchee, Safe Grabs, Ninu.

A *fourth* category of day-to-day opportunities comes from problems, which are not real, but **potential**. Our fears. That is the realm of **worries**, **concerns**, solved by products such as Bumpsters, Safetytat, Lisa Gable Accessories, Grayl, Objemer.

And *finally* there is the difference between going by and being **truly happy**. Between being merely content and feeling really well, fully satisfied. *Oscar Wilde* put it best: *most people just survive; to live is another matter.*

---

[4]All examples named here will be detailed in the next chapters.

That can happen through *socialization* (Miss O & Friends, Meet Me), improving one's *self-esteem* (Harry's, Gymshark, Vestiaire Collective), sense of *self-realization* (Jim's Career Academy of Hair Design), or simply *small daily treats* that bring moments of exquisite pleasure (Gousto, Nissin Foods).

The next chapter will go over these five sources of opportunities, and how best to organize to generate them.

Then the following chapter will focus on **inquire**. And by that is meant, before searching for a solution, performing **three types of tests** on the problem/opportunity:

- Does it pass the **time** test (two months as shall be seen)?
- **Isn't there** already a solution in the market I am unaware of?; and
- How **pervasive** is the problem: does it exist only for me, or instead my friends and acquaintances share my feelings about it?

Once the problem/opportunity passed these three tests, next is to find a **solution**.

And the emphasis here is in finding, not creating it anew, which can be done in one of **six** ways (Chapter 4):

1. Applying the **net** (Gorillas, Athelas, Too Good To Go);

2. Importing the solution that is already serving another type of **client/entity** (Redminut, Funk-tional, Fenty Beuty, Eyelights);

3. Adapting a solution that is being instrumental to another **need** (Crayon Holders, Hyper-Chiller, Lola Rola, TwistieMag, SockTabs);

4. Bringing the solution from another **place**, be it a different *distribution channel* or a distinct *geographical area* (Click n' Clean, Barbie, American Girl, Fresh Paper); and then still if none of the above can be found, the solution may very well lie in:

5. **Adding or deducting** (*quantitatively or qualitatively*) one or more characteristics of *a product/service already in the market* (Knix, Roller Buggy, StashAll, Fast Eddies, QB House); and finally

6. Buying an **existing patent**, which solves the problem, but has not been launched into the market.

It lies dormant to be bought by someone willing to (1) do a marketing plan, (2) assemble a team, (3) prepare operations, and (4) obtain the required financing. That is the difference between an inventor and an innovator, a technician/scientist and an entrepreneur. Examples are Readerest, the Bic pen, Tampax or Flyte.

Finally, there is the **A** of **Action**, the last letter of the word PISA, which stands for: (1) building a **prototype** (something that, as will be seen, is under the grasp of anyone[5] with flexible materials such as silicone, clay, or wax); (2) beginning the **early stages** of patenting the product; and bringing it to the market (3) **gradually** and (4) **minimizing the cost**.

Chapter 5 will also analyze two further issues: the importance of creating *a focus group* (in person or online) to continually update the product (The Ice Cream Canteen and Scrub Daddy are examples) and of having *a clear definition of failure* (the examples of Amazon, Disney, and Frito-Lay illustrate that such measures not only prevent unnecessary losses but can also be the origin of great successes).

---

[5]The seven-year-old Cassidy Crowley did that.

And so a last question arises, before moving onto the next chapters to detail the PISA method: why has the **PISA method** remained an **untold story** so far? The answer is twofold:

First, although producing highly valuable innovations, simplicity lacks the *glamour* of technical sophistication.

And *second, until recently there was no story to be told*: in order to value simplicity, one must be immersed in complexity—something that modern society in recent decades brought evermore. Thus, simplicity as a great source of innovations is an idea whose time has come.

Let's then turn to the next chapters and detail the quiet revolution underway. So quiet indeed that falling below the "radar" is unnoticed by some, but whose value makes the attention of all worthwhile.

CHAPTER 2

Opportunities That Come To Us in the Form of Problems (We Do Not Have to Look for Them)

Entrepreneurs are problem solvers.

Lisa Gable
(founder of L.G. Accessories)

2.0. Overview

The first step in PISA is to take into account the *opportunities* that daily life brings disguised as **problems**.

This requires organizing our daily life in a non-time-consuming way as described in Section 2.1.

Then Section 2.2 will distinguish among the five types of **problems** that constitute *opportunities*.

And Section 2.3 concludes by stressing a few points.

2.1. Acknowledging Opportunities in Daily Life

We want to be aware of *opportunities* without hurting our jobs, family life, and leisure.

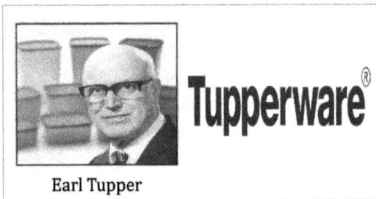
Earl Tupper

That requires first a simple *organization* and second a clear idea of what to *focus on*.

The organization has four components:

1. A *pen and pencil* in the pocket;
2. To *write down* the essential every time one comes across a problem (which should not take more than 15/30 seconds);
3. Then when at home to put the paper in a *drawer*; and
4. *Forget* about it for two months.

Tom Monaghan

Ideas are like birds: they fly and we tend to forget them. Thus it is important to write them down as soon as possible (and not only later when at home), following the advice of Earl Tupper (inventor of Tupperware) and of Tom Monaghan (cofounder of Domino's Pizza).

Socrates, the Greek philosopher, when questioned about what is more important, intelligence or memory, answered: *one knows only what one is able to remember.*

Later on, at home, one can then with time complete the essential of what was previously written in the piece of paper.

And putting it down in paper has the other advantage noted by Ben-Gurion (founder of Israel who was known for writing everything in meetings): *when writing down we structure our thoughts.*

Ben-Gurion

Finally, one should not act immediately upon the idea for three reasons (later developed in the next chapter when one will discuss the **I** of Inquire of PISA).

First, it is important to know **how frequent** the problem/opportunity is. *Second*, regardless of frequency, it is also relevant to evaluate after some time (e.g., two months) if we still do feel strongly about the problem or we do not attribute **importance** to it anymore. And *third*, it is advantageous to **compare** all ideas in order to select one, and only one, and thus enable focus.

So, (1) *pen*, (2) *paper*, (3) *drawer*, and… (4) *wait*. The time to look at, to evaluate, to select and act upon will come later.

But what should one write about? As said, we write about problems that come our way as we go about our lives.

No one enjoys problems. Thus those who solve them are welcome, opening the door for entrepreneurs as problem solvers, making of problems nothing more than opportunities in disguise.

That said, life brings **five** basic types of problems.

The *first* are **bothers, hassles, grievances.**

The *second* is the feeling of **disappointment** when using a product/service: the outcome falls short of expectations, the product is slightly "incompetent" and not quite up to the task and expectations.

The *third* type of problems are **complications**, complexity, lack of flexibility/versatility. To get the job done one must use several products, creating an opportunity for a multitask product.

Then *fourth,* there are the **concerns**, the worries, our fears. Although not real but only potential, they nevertheless pervade our lives.

Seneca

As Seneca, the Roman philosopher and statesman, once observed: *our fears outnumber our dangers.* And the former are frequently a product of our imagination. But since perception is reality, they do nevertheless affect us, creating anxiety.

And finally, there is the *fifth* type of problems: many people live day by day, they go by, they are content. But not **truly happy**, feeling well and fulfilled. Thus the opportunity for products/services that bring **joy** into people's lives.

Before the next section that will provide examples of these five types of problems that constitute opportunities, it is worthwhile to note that there are **three other sources of opportunities outside the scope of PISA.**

As per the last three lines of Figure 2, they respect either market changes or opportunities that must be created.

One example of market changes, **industries disruptions,** happened when many airlines **stopped** providing pillows and blankets during flights.

Opportunities Sources	Characteristics	Frequency	Technical complexity	
PROBLEMS	1 **Bothers** (aggravations)	High	Low	
	2 **Incompetent products** (not up to the task / short of some qualities)	High	Low	
	3 **Complications** (lack of flexibility)	High	Low	PISA Focus
	4 **Concerns** (worries)	High	Low	
	5 **Merely content** (not happy)	High	Low	
MARKET CHANGES	6 **Industries disruptions/unbalances**	?	?	Other types of opportunities
	7 **Crisis** (economy)	No	?	
CREATION	8 **Future** which has already happened	?	High	

Figure 2 PISA Focus: Five in eight types of opportunities

Angie Higa: **Sky Dreams**

First: fashionable	Blankets + Pillows	when airlines stopped providing

Then:	Full line for people on the go/move

Foldable blankets that convert into bags   Shopping totes   Purses   Fashion masks

Aloha collection

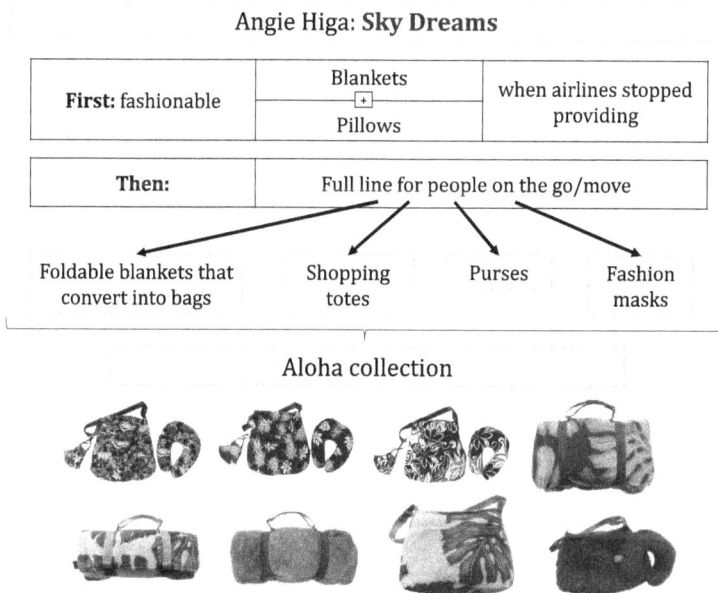

Figure 3 Industries disruptions

That led to the start-up **Sky Dreams** created by Angie Higa, which first sold (fashionable) blankets and pillows, and later extended its portfolio into other types of blankets (convertible into bags), shopping totes, purses, and fashion masks (Figure 3).

Still another type of industries disruptions is **unbalances**, be it shortages or surpluses, creating opportunities for intermediaries.

Too Good To Go is an example. Created in 2015 it is a mobile app that links restaurants with food surpluses to customers willing to buy them at a discount.

The restaurant creates *a magic box*, indicating its content and the price. Then the client after confirming the purchase picks it up. And Too Good To Go makes money with two fees: a fixed fee per order and a yearly one for administrative purposes.

Crisis (before last line in Figure 2) is another type of off-PISA opportunities. Dick Clark, former president of the pharmaceutical Merck, used to recall that Machiavelli recommended to Prince Lawrence of Florence *never to waste the opportunities created by a good crisis.*

During COVID, masks clouded the glasses until ... the solution came in terms of FogBlock (Figure 4).

Figure 4 FogBlock

Finally the last line of Figure 2 indicates the third type of opportunities untapped by the PISA method: **creating the future that has already happened**.

What that means is:

1. *Identifying* new trends;
2. That are *starting* to grow exponentially;
3. *Jumping* at the trend at an early stage; and thus
4. *Ahead* of most of the competition.

It is not necessary for firms to be the very first in the market (thus the innovators), much less having come up with the idea (being the inventors).

But they have to be **early adopters**, such as Elon Musk with Tesla (electric cars), Space X (low-cost rockets and spacecrafts), and Solar City (Sun energy panels), or as Steve Jobs with the smartphone whose technology—at the time of Apple's launch—existed already within Nokia; however, its engineers did not consider it ready because of the high price, something that Apple's success totally disproved.

To sum up, although important, these **three** types of opportunities (industries disruptions/unbalances, crisis, and the future that already happened) are nevertheless **outside** the scope of PISA, because they are either (1) more technologically *complex* (in the case of the future that already happened), (2) *less frequent* (crisis), or/and (3) *more marginal* to people's lives (industries disruptions and unbalances).

PISA focus on problems, which by being at the center of people's lives increase familiarity with them and so are related to the Maslow pyramid in Figure 5.

The examples of the next section will illustrate that bothers, incompetent products, and complications are related to Maslow's first-level pyramid.

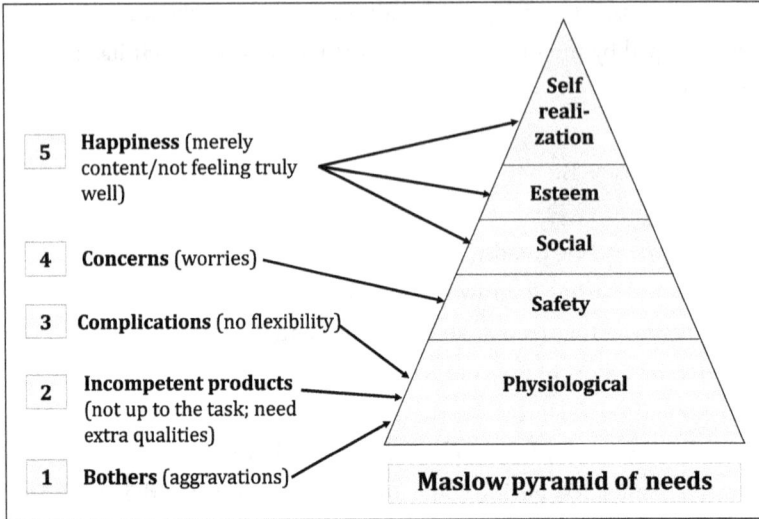

Figure 5 Opportunities are problems that come to us

Concerns relate to the second level. And true happiness can be increased either by satisfying social needs, self-esteem, or self-realization (third tier). Peter Drucker used to summarize the top three by saying that society should bring **status and function**.

2.2. The Five Types of Daily Problems That Are Sources of Great Opportunities

2.2.1. Bothers

Major inconveniences follow us all day long. Therefore, there is the need for **solutions** that minimize or erase them.

It starts at breakfast with a *transparent toaster* (which comes in glass or strong plastic), enabling us to see if the toast is just as we want it. At the point.

Then when preparing the tea, tap water contains limestone that ends up in the cups. The innovation here was *to add to kettles a mouth filter*, a net, which prevents the limestone from passing through.

Still before leaving home frequently one takes the laundry out of the machine. Pairing and even losing[6] socks used to be a problem until *SockTabs* came along: they are essentially simple pins made of plastic to avoid rusting and damaging the socks. The company is valued at over $1 million (in 2023).

And grooming is facilitated by home delivered personal hygiene products (both for men and women) either by *Harry's* or by *Dollar Shave Club*.

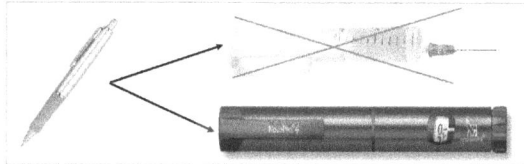

When going out many ladies carry in their purses *Funk-tional*, a low-priced and highly flexible footwear similar to those used by ballet dancers and that they can change into, from heeled footwear, when needed.

Anyone suffering from type one diabetes,[7] instead of syringes that create a self-image of sickness, can use *Novo-Pen*, which with the shape of a pen performs the same function.

---

[6]With socks frequently ending up inside the pockets of garments.
[7]Sometimes in type one diabetes besides regular insulin injections, there may be the occasional need for additional doses when blood sugar levels are high.

If traveling, bags may include *Warby Parker* designer glasses, which after being virtually tried are home delivered at a convenient price; and *Cooltan* swimwear that allows sunshine to go through the tissue enabling for a uniform tan in all the body; or still *Athletic Greens*: a great tasting drink with a complex blend of 75 vitamins and minerals. Without artificial colors and sweeteners it meets all the body's daily needs and thus the market made the company a unicorn.

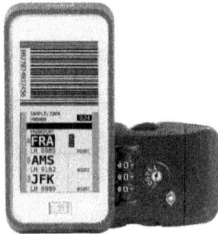

And whenever flying with checked luggage one can forgo the hassle of checking in baggage at the airport with *Bagtag*. The system with an electronic bag tag and two apps (one at the customer's mobile and the other at the airline system) allows the passenger to proceed digitally just as when checking in plane seats: Lufthansa, Swissair, KLM, Austrian, China Southern are some of the airlines that have joined the system invented by the Dutch Erik Harkes.

At home, the constant hassle of ensuring that children do their homework has been soothed with *Pencil Bugs*, an invention by nine-year-old Jason O'Neill.

The above examples illustrate **how "small" innovations make great differences** in bringing comfort to people's lives. And there are many other illustrations of simple, nonsophisticated goods that, by eliminating or at least minimizing bothers, make life easier and therefore happier: the *Post-it* (which is basically paper with glue); the *clips*; the *multicolor pen*; *Liquid Paper* (white corrector); the *Kleenex*; the *band-aid* (basically gauze plus glue tape);[8] *Tupperware*; the *TRX* (initially made of parachute leftovers strong enough to sustain body-weight); Bizchair.com (a site which offers low prices and large variety in furniture); *Vibram Five Fingers*

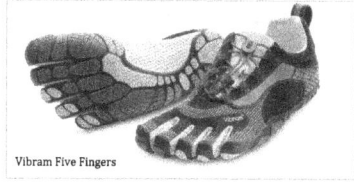

Vibram Five Fingers

(footwear that with the format of fingers gives the sensation of walking barefoot); *golf clubs* (e.g., putters) for left-handers;[9] or *Shareswell*.

The latter solved the problem for newlyweds of having to return unwanted gifts to the stores or accepting money as presents, which, in some cultures, is considered inappropriate.

Emily Washkowitz solved the problem by creating a **platform** where:

   1st—The bride and groom register;
   2nd—Indicate the type of stocks they are interested in;
   3rd—The guests choose the stocks they want to offer;
   4th—Guests choose a stockbroker in the website;
   5th—Guests send the money;
   6th—The stocks are bought and placed in the bride and groom's account.

Indeed, life is full of small inconveniences that become great opportunities. And their frequency transforms them from simple inconveniences into major aggravations.

Where did I put my keys? (solution: stick them to the fridge, but how?); computer cables are always so messy (solution: tie them but with what?); the pacifier keeps falling to the ground (solution: use something to pin it to the shirt); how to make sure my children see the message I'm leaving (solution: glue a message to the door with scotch tape…).

---

[8]Substituting four previous tasks: (1) gauze; (2) cutting it; (3) tightening around the wound; and (4) placing the adhesive.

[9]10 to 15 percent of the world population is left-handed and requires golf clubs with reversed heads. Yearly sales are close to $4 billion.

One solution for all problems? Or a single one for a multitude of them? A simple organizer and fixer?

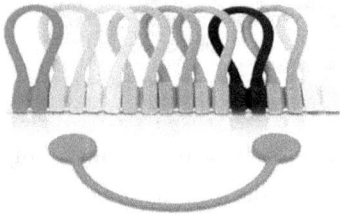

TwistieMag is a (1) magnet + (2) of plastic + (3) flexible that can solve all the above.

And age plays no role in the entrepreneurs' capacity of solving daily problems.

As sometimes the conditions at sea do not allow for surfing, the **Hamborg** teenagers found the solution by creating the *Hamboards*: inspired by skates, they are wheeled surfboards that simulate in land the sensation of sea surfing.

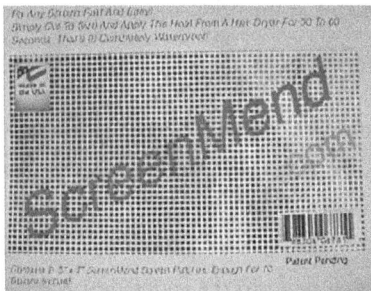

ScreenMend? It is a patch to repair mosquito nets, invented by nine-year-old **Lily Hooks**. It consists of a piece of net with wax that softens when heated with a hair dryer. The patch is placed on the mosquito net and when the wax cools, it solidifies, thus becoming strongly glued.

2.2.2. Incompetent Products

The second major source of daily problems is products that are **not quite** up to the task. Performing their function reasonably, their use nevertheless creates a sensation of disappointment. That an extra quality is lacking. That sensation is a source of innovation and **opportunity**.

Type of new quality / Technology / Where	Simple	Average complexity
Within the product	Elevators Sleep Styler	GoPro
Adjacent to the product	Drop Stop (seat gap filler) Soundbender	Ice Cream Canteen

Figure 6 Types of incompetent products: What is missing

Examples in **Figure 6** are Elevators, The Sleep Styler, the Drop Stop (gap seat filler), Soundbender, GoPro, and Ice Cream Canteen.

This type of innovation differs on how basic the technology is and whether the new quality(ies) is(are) added to the product itself or adjacent to it. However, the basic question that triggers the innovation is always the same: **what is missing?**

Elevators is a brand of shoes. While most clients select footwear with the criteria of comfort, design, and price, others however look for another sparsely provided qual-ity: *how taller do the shoes make me look?*

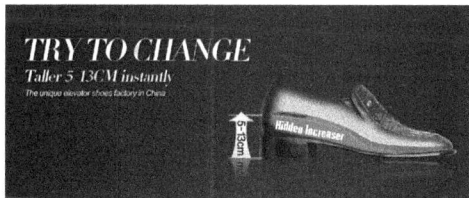

That was the opportunity seized by *Elevators*, which provides shoes with a hidden height increase of between 5 and 13 cm (2 to 5 inches).

That innovation has the further advantage of price being a nonissue. Indeed, the consumer's sole concern is looking taller. Everything else? Secondary or almost nonexistent.

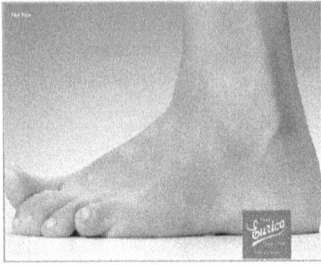

Also *Eurico* is a brand serving exclusively women and men with large feet (in the United States over size 9 and size 10, respectively, and in Europe over size 40 and size 43, respectively), making another bother go away: walking into a store and looking for large enough shoes. Now I know simply which brand to ask for.

The long time it takes to curl hair is the problem solved by *The Sleep Styler*, a hands-free system to use while one sleeps. Consisting of a plush roller that straightens and curls the hair effortlessly, it can be used when eating, watching TV, or even … sleeping.

The hair rollers are super absorbent, heat free, and made of yoga towel fabric that dries the hair fast while the foam inside ensures comfort.

The result? Within one year the entrepreneur **Tara Brown** took an idea she got while fixing her daughter's hair to $100 million in sales and a $15 million worth company.

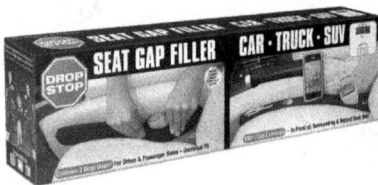

Newburguer almost killed a side walker and hit a lamp post while driving and at the same time trying to grab his mobile that had fallen in-between his front seat and the central console.

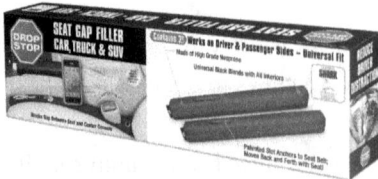

The "incompetence" here being the seat gaps, the solution is a simple block of polyester (to guarantee flexibility to adapt to any car) covered with neoprene (and thus elegance, smoothness, and impermeability). The product (*Drop Stop*)

was adopted by the Los Angeles Police Department and the company achieved $24 million in sales in four years and was worth $5 million.

Soundbender is another example of an accessory that bridges a major product shortcoming: laptop sound is emitted from the top, directed away from the user. Thus … Soundbender: simply a magnetic plastic device in the shape of a shell, greatly amplifying the sound and creating a business worth $1.3 million.

Nick Woodman's problem was distinct. An enthusiast of radical sports, he made a point of sharing his experiences on visual social media. That meant using rubber bands to tie a disposable camera to his wrist. However, even when done in the best possible way, it was nothing more than a mediocre solution.

The solution was *GoPro*: the world's most versatile camera for videos and photos when surfing, parachuting, mountaineering, moto crossing, and any radical sport.

Its qualities are (1) semi-professional quality, (2) waterproof, (3) resistant, and (4) easy to tie.

The inner technology of the camera existed already, but the added new accessory characteristics created a unicorn of $4 billion.

There is an old German proverb "des geschmack ist unbestreibar" (tastes are not to be discussed) that applies easily to ice creams with their hundreds of brands and varieties.

In common, they last only for a short time because within a few minutes of the purchase they start melting and losing flavor, something delayed but far from being solved by travel coolers.

That problem is solved by the *Ice Cream Canteen*. In the size of pints, a stainless-steel pot creating vacuum guarantees that the ice cream stays frozen for four hours, ideal for picnics or long trips.

In short, product incompetence is a never-ending source of opportunities as products are never perfect.

And so, the introduction presented the unicorn *Spanx*: footless body shaping pantyhoses that extend only to mid-leg length, solved the problem of visible seams when wearing sandals or open shoes.

However, another problem remained: due to its very thin texture the pantyhoses could be easily cut or torn.

Again, an unsolved problem is an untapped opportunity. And so *Sheertex* came along, claiming to be for all purposes unbreakable. They withstand even if pulled with the upmost force of bare hands, and resist snags from toenails or safety pins. They even endure the washing machine.

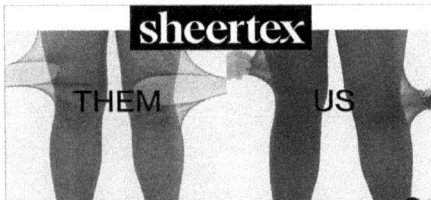

A great product, but as perfection is inexistent, opportunities remain.

In the case of Sheertex the main problem is the price, as it is far more expensive than the $5 price of a drugstore standard hose pair. And a control-top model is still more expensive, slightly scratchier than Spanx and not as fancy as other brands.

Thus while the main quality of Sheertex is being indestructible in human hands, other brands stand out in **other qualities**. Although all improve, the remaining imperfections together with customers' ever higher expectations represent market opportunities.

2.2.3. The Search for Simplicity

The increasing sophistication of life requires that more and more tasks must be performed.

Specialized tools enable performance. However, complexity increases with the number of tools. Thus the need for **multitask products**, regardless of the consumer: ladies, men, teenagers, or children (**Figure 7**).

Day2Night, one shoe with five (removable) heels, replaces the need to travel with several pairs of shoes.

Examples	Ladies	Men	Teenagers	Children
Shoe heels	Day2Night			
	Tanya Heath			
Purse pockets	Pouchee			
Perfumes	Ninu			
Oversized blanket sweatshirt	The Comfy			
Hot pot grabber	SafeGrabs			
Towel/change clothes / blanket / sleeping bag / pillow neck	Chawel			
Pillows which double as stuffed animals				Pillow Pets

Figure 7 The need for multitask products

And *Tanya Heath* goes one step forward, providing heels in different colors and designs.

As different ladies' purses are used for distinct occasions, it creates the major inconvenience of having to transfer the contents among purses that frequently differ in their number of pockets. That is what *Pouchee*, a bag to be inserted within purses, solved. And it can also be used as a purse itself.

Ninu is the world's first smart perfume. Using the smartphone one can select the type, amount, and mixtures of fragrances in dozens of alternatives according to the occasion, weather, season, or feel.

Comfy is a one-size-fits-all oversized hood that can be used as a coat, blanket, or pillow. And its very large pocket keep hands warm and stores phones, snacks, keys, and so on.

To take hot pots out of ovens or microwaves, a grab is needed. *SafeGrabs* fulfills this need besides being a table towel, food cover, microwave mat, and jar opener, which are its **five (in one)** functions. At its core, it is a simple round silicone mat, yet with $4 million in annual sales, it has built a company valued at $10 million.

Changing clothes in beaches involved the difficult and uncomfortable task of wrapping a towel around the bodies. Until *Chawel* came: a double towel untied at one side and with a head opening on the other.

And again a **five-in-one product**: besides clothes change, it can be used as a beach towel, sleeping bag, blanket (for camping), and neck pillow for airplanes.

The wish of her children to use stuffed animals as bed pillows was a constant strain on Jennifer Telfer that she decided to solve by using pillows that **double** as stuffed animals and thus creating a $5 million revenue business (*Pillow Pets*).

Multitask goods, bringing an *extra quality* to an existing product, or directly addressing an *unsolved problem* are **three types of opportunities** that respect the bottom layer of the Maslow pyramid in Figure 5 (opportunities number one, two, and three).

But there are two other important layers in the pyramid: **concerns** (number 4) and what brings **true happiness** (number 5). Let's start with worries.

2.2.4. Concerns/Worries

We are here in the realm of the potential, the eventual, not the real, actual. Nevertheless, a source of inquietude.

Which starts right at the beginning of life with feeding babies. The sharp edge of spoons is a danger. And the unwillingness of many newborns to eat an inquietude. They nevertheless have their favorite toys in the form of elephants and other animals.

So why not add to a silicone toy elephant a round spoon and use that for baby feeding?

And so *Baby Toon* is born. No sharp edges. Soft (made of silicone). The short spoon makes it impossible to go deep into the mouth. Easy to grab. And that doubles as a toy since besides being funny it comes in different colors and animals.

Baby Toon was invented by **seven-year-old Cassidy Crowley**, creating a $1 million worth business.

When in bed another source of concern is babies bumping their heads against the wood.

And lining the beds with clothes creates the danger of babies suffocating by sucking the protection clothes. The solution came with *Bumpsters*, a protective cover made from porous material created by mom **Sarah Barker**. It allows protection against head bumping and avoids suffocation.

The saying that children are a problem which never stops growing is exemplified by the risk that when they start walking, they can get easily lost in crowded environments.

Thus *Safetytat*, temporary safety tattoos that do not come out with water, but that after a couple of days naturally fades away. It enables parents to write their mobile number when at a beach, swimming pool, or theme parks. And to remind schoolteachers of allergies or medicines that must be taken.

And as worries accompany people throughout life, they are a constant source of opportunities.

Grayl is a water purifier for camping, tracking, and mountaineering, which enables to drink water from any source found in nature. Without any concern.

The *Larq bottle filtered* is an alternative. Designed in the shape of a bottle, it filters water from any source, removing pesticides, chemicals, and bacteria.

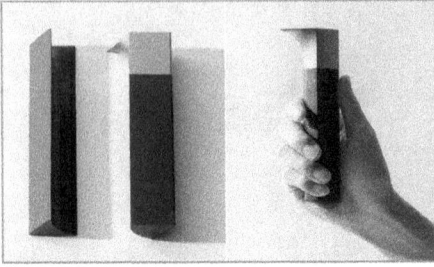

The *Objemer* is a glass breaker (that doubles as a makeshift hammer) specially designed to carry in cars in case of accidents.

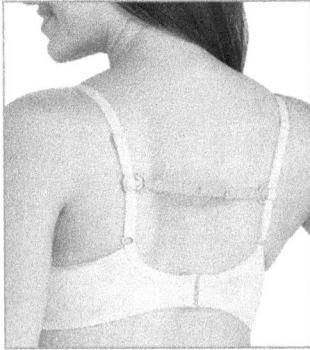

Lisa Gable when 67 years old created a cloth strip linking the bras straps to prevent the bras from moving and so becoming a source of discomfort and concern. That was the first product of the company L.G. Accessories.

Am I taking enough vitamins and minerals? Simply put: one more thing to worry about when eating during the day, instead of simply selecting what gives me pleasure, the treat I deserve.

So, as mentioned before, the solution lies in having at every breakfast *Athletic Greens*: a great tasting drink that is a complex of **75 vitamins and minerals** without any artificial **colors and sweeteners**.

In other words, the equivalent of 75 pills freeing from health concerns during the day. The result? A **unicorn**.

2.2.5. True Happiness

David Thoreau noted that *the mass of men live lives of quiet desperation.* They go by. At best content. But seldom feeling truly fulfilled and **happy**. They survive. To live, as has been said, is another matter.

Thus the opportunity to bring into people's lives (by order of increasing importance): (1) *small treats*; (2) *socialization*; (3) *self-esteem*; and (4) *self-realization*.

Examples of *treats* are the **unicorns** *Gousto* and *Nissin Foods*.

Gousto is a British meal kit retailer that delivers box kits at consumers' doorsteps, among 55 recipe options per week.

Nissin Foods, another great success, is a precooked instant noodles requiring only pouring hot water.

Gymshark, still another unicorn, is both a treat and improves one's self-esteem as it offers (1) affordable gym wear that (2) makes people look great. Francis, one of the two founders (both aged 20), dropped out of university, stopped working as a delivery driver for Pizza Hut, and started manufacturing the garments in his parents' garage as taught by his mother.

The need for *socialization* is behind the success of so many chat sites, be they (e.g.) only for girls (*Miss O & Friends*), founded by Julliette Brindak when she was 16 years old, or for teenagers of both sexes: the brothers Catherine and Dave Cook (when 15 and 16 years old, respectively) founded and sold the site *Meet Me* for $100 million.

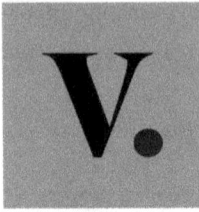

V. Also contributing to self-esteem is the unicorn *Vestiaire Collective*, an online platform to trade second-hand luxury fashion products: from clothes to shoes to bags to jewelry, brands like Dior, Celine, or Chanel are sold at up to 70 percent discount.

Founded in a small apartment in Paris and selling initially garments provided by friends, the company today employs 400 people in 90 countries and offers three million items to nine million members.[10]

Another example of how to contribute to *self-realization* is companies that contribute to charity according to sales.

Harry's is a unicorn founded by **Jeff Raider** with basically the same business model of Dollar Shave Club: home delivery of grooming products thus supplying both convenience and low price.

Initially it donated blades for veterans of Afghanistan and Iraq on a one (sale) to one (free) basis.

Later it shifted its philanthropy policy to 1 percent of sales and allowed employees every year five days of paid time to work at an NGO of their choice.

And naturally start-ups that focus on training can also contribute to self-realization. That is the case of **Jim Butenschoen** who founded *Career Academy of Hair Design* when he was 65 years of age (**Figure 8**).

---

[10]Any product that makes the consumer feel responsible or smart also contributes to self-esteem. Examples are Tesla and all other electric car brands, solar panels, or even "smart" chandeliers that collect the melted candles into a tube to double extend candle life (*Benjamin Shine Candles*).

Not NGOs / How	Need	Social	Esteem	Self-realization	Small pleasures
P R O D U C T	Miss O & Friends	Yes			
	Meet me	Yes			
	Jim's academy			Yes	
	Gousto				Yes
	Nissin foods				Yes
Accessory added automatic	Harry's shave veterans program (one-one/ 1%)		Yes	Yes	
	Spanx	Yes	Yes		
	Gymshark	Yes	Yes		
	Tesla	Yes	Yes		

Figure 8 Contributions to happiness

2.3. Summary

Contrary to this chapter examples, the world is full of innovations, which apparently have everything to succeed. They are technically sophisticated. And quite new, distinct from every other product.

Yet they fail. Because they lack the **fundamental**: people **caring** about the problem they solve.

It is not so much that they fail to solve the problem (that they are incompetent), it is that they solve nonexistent problems (they do well the useless).

Juicero? A Wi-Fi connected juice machine at the price of $400. No one cared about.

Parrot pot? An ingenious idea. The pot indicates the amount of water, sunlight, and heat the plant is receiving ($170). People couldn't care less.

And **Eye** is a case that is also a phone strapped to another phone to create two phones: one for the day (work) and another for the night (personal). At the reasonable price of $190. Result? There was no demand.

These among many other examples illustrate that **the starting point of innovations must be a problem**. Something that is either a real nuisance or even an aggravation. In any case an actual obstacle to well-being. To feeling happy.

So, the **PISA method starts** with not an idea, not an invention, but with a **problem**, an actual, factual need. Something out there bothering us.

And they can be of **five** types:

1. **Grievances** (for instance, the ache caused by high-heeled shoes creating the success of Funk-tional or the hassle of checking in luggage
   at airport solved by BagTag);
2. **Underperformed** tasks by products that fall short of some required
   quality (thus the opportunity for Soundbender in laptops);
3. Lack of **simplicity** due to the increasing sophistication of modern
   life (creating a need for multitask products such as Day2Night or
   SafeGrabs);
4. **Concerns/worries**, which although only potential, only fears,
   nevertheless affect people's lives (and consequently the need for
   Bumpsters, Safetytat, or Grayl); and finally
5. Goods that either provide daily moments of gratification (e.g., Gousto)
   or improve the overall sense of **happiness** (Jim's hair academy).

Sure, one can also innovate through **untapped needs** (Facebook, Insta-
gram) or **jumping into the early stages of a growing trend** (electric cars,
solar energy).[11]

---

[11]As illustrated in Figure 2.

But those are not the only way to produce **unicorns**, as demonstrated by the previous examples of applying the PISA method: Spanx, Rent the Runway, Dollar Shave Club, Harry's, Warby Parker, GoPro, Gousto, Vestiaire Collective, Gymshark, Athletic Greens, and so on.

And PISA generally requires lower investment, is much simpler, and has higher probability of success. Apple is idolized and much deservedly so. But it nevertheless counted innumerous failures: Lisa, Macintosh, Apple 3, Cube, iPod hi-fi, to name only a few.

In short, to innovate, it is better to start with a problem detected in daily life. And which "asks" and "begs" for a solution.

Chapter 4 will discuss that such a solution **does not need** to be constructed, since frequently it already exists being applied elsewhere: in another part of reality and so only adaptation is needed.

But before doing so, there is a **word of caution** that one must address: is the identified problem just a nuisance or a *real grievance*?

And if so, how do *other people* feel about it? Are we the only one or is the feeling general, shared by many?

That is what must be inquired next. And that is the I of the PISA method we turn to in the next chapter.

CHAPTER 3

Inquiring Through Emotions and Actions (Never Mind Thoughts and Words)

People do not act as they say, do not say what they think, do not think what they feel, but act as they feel.

David Ogilvy

3.0. Overview

The previous chapter analyzed how to find **opportunities**.

However, before investing time, energy, and money in search for a solution it makes sense to ask: **how important is it?**

For such a purpose **five** inquiries are helpful:

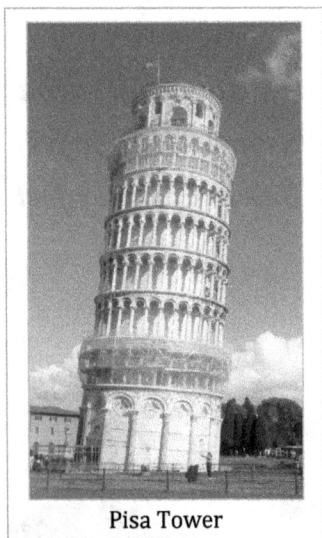

Pisa Tower

1. Does the opportunity pass the test of **time**?
2. In which opportunity should one **focus** on (in case more than one opportunity was found)?
3. How to **describe in detail** the nature of the problem (to make sure the solution will get the job done)?
4. Isn't there already somewhere (e.g., in some specialized distribution channel) a **solution** that I am not aware of?; and finally
5. How do **others** feel about the problem? Is it general or not so much?

3.1. Does the Problem Pass the Test of Time?

The first PISA step in the previous chapter was to write down in a piece of paper the problem (be it a bother, a product incompetence, a complication, whatever) one comes across in daily life and then put it away in a drawer for **two months**.

That prevents being a weathercock constantly changing directions.

Now, (e.g.) two months later, time has come to open the drawer, look at all the pieces of paper, and ask *two basic questions*:

First, **after time** has passed, how do I **feel** about the problem? Still upset, or has time weathered its importance?

Now, does it feel as a mere inconvenience or still an aggravation? Something to be lived with, or worthwhile of my time, energy, and money in finding a solution to make it go away?

Depending upon the answer, one shrugs it off or one keeps the paper. That is the **time test**, as time does not respect what it does not participate into.

The second question is to ask how **frequent** is the problem? During the two months period, did it happen only once or occurred **repeatedly**?

Both answers allow to place the opportunities in a diagram as in **Figure 9** (illustrated with some of previous chapter examples), according to the frequency (horizontal axis) and importance (vertical axis) of each opportunity.

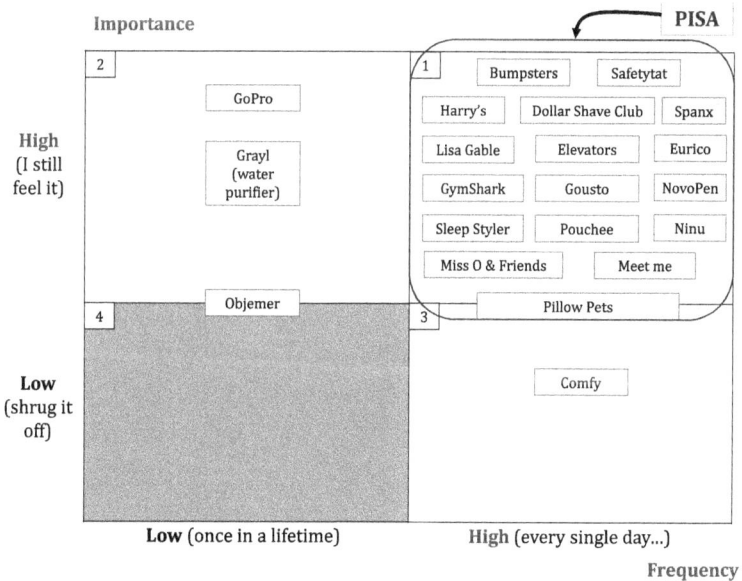

Figure 9 Evaluating problems in terms of importance and frequency

Note: The location of each problem is a mere example, hypothetical.

The objective is to select the best in both or in the balance of the two axes. The more a problem is located at the right top side of the figure (northeast), the more it is indeed a **real opportunity** and not a simple **distraction**.

And it is advantageous to **focus** on **one** and only one. Why?

3.2. The Importance of Focus

The saying that *one should not put all eggs in a single basket* is as old as wrong.

Simple common sense dictates that the probability of breaking eggs increases with the number of baskets one carries.[12]

A man who chases two rabbits catches neither.
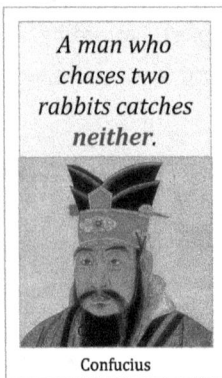
Confucius

Multibasket carriers are prone to disaster. And so the best way to avoid breaking eggs is to have a *single basket* and grab it firmly with both hands.

But besides that general principle, there are however other reasons to have a **single-tasking mindset**.

For some it will be the *first time* they launch an innovation. Even if not, since solutions differ, benefits of experience are narrow. Frequently innovations are done as a *complement to* other activities: a job and family care. And finally, innovation is *time* consuming, requiring that a solution be found elsewhere and adapted (next chapter) and then acted upon by building a prototype, improving it with a focus group, applying for a patent, and gradually launching into the market (Chapter 5).

---

[12]Also a favorite saying of Andrew Carnegie, the American entrepreneur.

Thus the importance of selecting the **one and only one** innovation that ranks best *in frequency* and *relevance* in the northeast corner of Figure 9.

And here there are two possibilities. First, if no problem ranks high in both axes, then one goes back to stage one of paper plus pencil (previous chapter), thus saving time, energy, and money. *Sometimes the best deals are those that are never made.*

However, if one problem/opportunity stands out in both dimensions, then one can move into the next section of this chapter.

3.3. Defining Well the Problem

School evaluates by the answers given. Life, foremost, by the questions asked. Because questions lead to the important.

Having the right answer (solution) to the wrong problem (question) is useless. The solution may be on target, but if the latter was badly defined, the former becomes irrelevant.

> *Questions are more important than answers.*

P. Drucker

A zero worth question with a 100 percent solution produces nothing ($0 \times 100 = 0$). But a 100 percent (on-target) question, even if only worth half of a solution (0.5) generates 50 percent ($100 \times 0.5 = 50$).

Thus a good question is almost half an answer (**Francis Bacon**) and consequently a man should be judged by his questions, not by his answers (**Voltaire**).

In the PISA case, when inquiring, a fundamental question is, What are the subdivisions of the problem, its main composing parts?

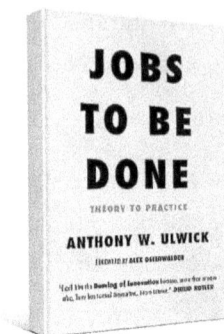

That is the subject of the book *Jobs To Be Done*, both useful for intrapreneurship (innovation within large corporations) and entrepreneurship (start-ups).

One starts with the fundamental question of **what job does the customer want to be done?** And its scope.

Defining the job *too narrowly* will limit the discovery of innovations and open the door to competition in the fringes. A too broad answer will result in a nonpractical task.

So the objective is to discover the entirety of the job the client wishes accomplished without falling into the accessory: first things first, second things never (P. Drucker).

One way to make sure one finds all the main requirements that the solution must meet, all the qualities it must have, is to go into a sequence of why to why to why…, until one is satisfied with the level of detail.

For example, a stove-top kettle user tries to boil water. But that is just a step to the ultimate goal of preparing a hot beverage to drink.

And so the latter opens the door for an innovation like *Keurig*, which gets the total job done on a simple platform.

Let's take the last chapter example of *Pouchee* (the common bag to put inside all ladies' handbags). What is the immediate problem? Answer: the purse's inside is a mess.

But why messy? Some bags have no pockets; and the number of pockets varies from bag to bag. That creates the problem of time in replacing items from one bag to the other.

So? Either one uses only one bag (something obviously out of the question for many ladies) or one separates the exterior (which varies) from the interior (to be kept constant) of handbags. Thus: *Pouchee.*

Rent the Runway is another example of innovation that became a unicorn, because it tapped all parts/aspects of the problem.

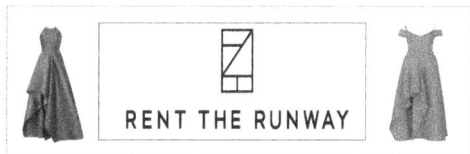

Highly priced designer dresses, the frequency of events, and the will to go to each event wearing a different dress (the need for variety) are solved by renting the dress instead of buying.

And also the risk of how will I look like? is alleviated with the money back policy; that of will I fit in? by sending two consecutive sizes of the same dress; and the option of buying afterwards satisfies the need for endowment, namely the possibility of "I falling in love with the dress" and thus finding hard to let it go.

In short, before moving on, it is fundamental to have a **detailed description of the entire job to be done**, the goal being to define all causal factors that contribute to performance.

3.4. What Do People Presently Do About the Problem?

Such a question is important for **two** reasons.

Sometimes it avoids the Brazilian saying of "raining in the wet" (to open open doors): sometimes the *solution already exists,* it is out there, but we simply missed it. Thus the question: *what am I missing?*

Other times the solution is nonexistent, but customers resign themselves to a *poor substitute*, whose awareness is nevertheless important to stress the characteristics that our solution must have in order to make a real difference.

3.4.1. Is There Already a Solution Somewhere That I Am Missing?

Such a thorough search is more important when the idea or problem I come across is related to an unusual activity. For instance, if one decides for the first time in a long while to go **on a picnic or spend a weekend camping**.

Novelty always creates a great number of ideas, which probably never before occurred, only that,… fortunately for consumers and unfortunately for entrepreneurs, frequently there is already a product addressing them.

Starting with food and drink, the first priority is to keep hydrated. Naturally that one brings water. But what if more water is needed? Well, the already mentioned *Grayl* and *Larq*, two distinct bottle-shaped water purifiers, are already available, enabling to take water from any source.

Then, to facilitate drinking there is a three-in-one *Camelbak* fusion reservoir: a backpack, plus an inserted bottle, plus a straw.

We may need a table. Light (1.8 kg). But allowing for a heavy load (10 kg). Preferably solar heated to charge the laptops, cell phones, tablets, and other electronic devices. Best still if it is water and rain proof. And finally great if it can be easily folded into the side pocket of a backpack. Its name is *Raddy Solar*.

Although we bought ice cream, there is nothing to worry about it melting. *Ice Cream Canteen* preserves it frozen for four hours.

As soon as we stop for the picnic, kids start running and creating havoc including trying to climb trees. Wouldn't it be great if there was something safe to help them, just as there are tools to help professionals climb poles?

Well, it exists already and the simplest starts at $50. The name is *Strap-On Tree Climbing Shoe Claws*.

If one stays outdoors overnight one needs towels, sleeping bags, warm jackets, and a tent.

And here there are several innovations, which offer all those functions in a single product with increasing degrees of sophistication.

Chawel, besides being a beach towel, garment to change clothes, and airplane pillow, is also a blanket and a sleeping bag (five in one).

Price Jones also serves both as a blanket and as a sleeping bag, but the latter comes with a pillow.

Doppelganger doubles as a sleeping bag and a jacket or long coat, coming with detachable parts that can easily be put together with zippers.

RhinoWolf is a lightweight gear that is simultaneously a tent, a sleeping bag, and a mattress.

Then still, *EastStorm* can be used as a blanket or a heat-retaining (90 percent), waterproof and windproof sleeping bag or tent. It also serves to reflect heat, form a radiation barrier, and send emergency signals.

For hygiene there is the *Mikihat* travel toothbrush made of environmentally friendly materials and whose case may be disassembled into two mouthwash cups, or used to store other products such as cosmetics and even small towels.

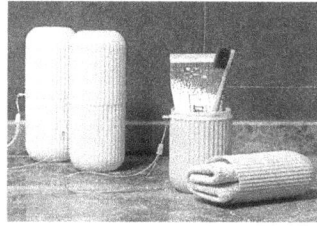

And for showering there is the *Wocream* solar camping shower with a 25 liters capacity and a button to adjust the size of the waterflow. After three hours of direct sunlight exposure the water temperature reaches 45°C.

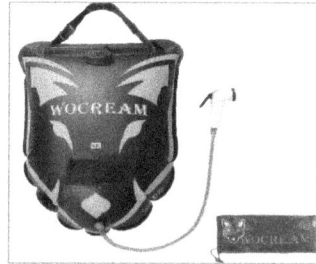

Finally security is guaranteed by the *XTPower* backpack or the *SOS rescue watch*.

The former is kitted out with solar panels that convert sunlight into solar energy stored in a battery pack that charges the smartphone.

And if one is at a remote place where there is no mobile phone network, the *O-Boy SOS* device is the solution developed by **Hadrien Dorchy** after a windsurfing accident that nearly cost him his life.

While at the coast of Cape Verde he lost his windsurfing board fin over a mile from the shore. Unable to return to the beach owing to the strong currents, Hadrien was adrift for more than five hours before a passing boat that was out for a night dive saved his life.

Determined to put his luck to good use, Hadrien created the O-Boy, the first wearable device with an in-built satellite transmitter, capable of transmitting SOS messages where there is no mobile phone network.[13]

And so on. The above sample of (15) camping/outdoors innovations, simply, illustrates that **the world has been around for a long time before an idea comes to us**.

Thus rather than going straight into creating a new gadget, prudence and common sense advise to carefully double check what is available out there. Starting with the internet. Then with general stores. And finally inspecting specialized distribution channels, by walking around and casually asking an employee: I am in need of so and so … what do you have? Nothing? Or a poor solution?[14]

3.4.2. What Are the Poor Solutions?

To become aware of poor solutions is also very useful as they enable to draw a fully detailed list of what is at present missing to get the job done.

Beaches and swimming pools frequently attract mosquitos, flies, and other insects, leading to the use of sprays, which of course is (1) *cumbersome*, (2) *smells*, (3) *bothers others*, and (4) there is the *fear of cancer*.

The above is a full description of the job to be done undertaken by *Enamorata*: a towel imbibed with an insect repellent. Its first quality is *practicality*; second it is *smelless*; third it *bothers* no one; and fourth the label guarantees *no risk* of cancer or any type of skin disease.

---

[13]The O-Boy sends out satellite distress signals from anywhere on Earth at the push of a button and being worn on the wrist, withstands impact and extreme conditions.
[14]Net communities must be managed with care as they create the risk of disclosure.

Indeed all product incompetences are both sources of opportunities and inspiration for the qualities solutions must have. As long as a problem remains unsolved, there is room for innovation.

Heat sensitivity is a frequent consequence for people with multiple sclerosis. Most specially in the breast.

Thus *Evian* launched a water bra. It did cool off, but besides leaking, the weight makes its use uncomfortable.

So what are the alternatives people recur to? Cool compresses, icepacks, cooling vests or wraps, and even dressing for heat with lightweight clothing. These are the poor substitutes upon which one must improve.

3.4.3. In Short

If the solution is **already** out there in some very specialized distribution channel, there is no room for innovation. At most and eventually for a joint venture helping to improve the marketing: after all why didn't we know about it? Why weren't we aware of its existence?

And if customers use a **poor solution**, or do nothing, that raises the issue of how important is the problem for them? Does it really matter? Do they truly care?

3.5. Looking at Others

Am I the *only one* concerned about the problem or part of a *huge crowd*?

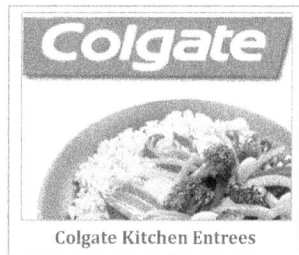

Colgate Kitchen Entrees

To inquire into the **pervasiveness** of the problem is fundamental before trying to solve it.

Harley Davidson Perfume

Something to be undertaken under the observation of the great marketeer David Ogilvy: **people do not act as they say; do not say what they think; do not think what they feel; but act as they feel.**

New Coke

In other words better to tap into (people's) **actions** and **feelings**, not **words** and **thoughts**, as multiple market research failures attest: from Colgate Kitchen entrees to Harley Davidson perfumes and Thirsty Dog bottled water, McDonald's arch deluxe, Crystal Pepsi, Apple's digital camera, or Microsoft Zune (an iPod competitor). Not to mention of course the best known of all: the New Coke.

Thirsty Dog bottled water

To test **actions** (not *words*), one can use **behavioral interviews**. And to test **emotions** (not *thoughts*), there is the **direct emotional assessment.**

3.5.1. Behavioral Interviews

Behavioral questions, without disclosing the intention of launching a product, focus on **past behavior**. One assumes that what one did in the past is the best predictor of what will be the actions in the future. *That the past is prologue.*[15]

---

[15]Inscription in the tomb of Tutankhamun.

For instance, to evaluate **Ninu**[16] (the multiple perfume scents) some of the following **behavioral questions** would be useful:

- How many perfumes do you **use**?
- How often do you **change** your scent:
  More than once per day?
  Daily?
  Several times a week?
  Once a week?
  Several times a month?
  None?

- Do you usually carry different perfumes in your **handbag** or keep them **nearby** (in drawers at work, your car, and so on) to **change** them as you see fit?
  Always?
  Often?
  Sometimes?
  Rarely?
  Never?

- **How many** perfumes on average do you carry in your bag?

The assumptions underlying these questions are that **the need for Ninu** is greater, (1) the larger the *average number* of perfumes people use, (2) the *frequency* at which they change scent, and (3) *how many* different perfumes they carry with them in their handbags all day long.

---

[16]The innovation of the world's first smart perfume was discussed in the previous chapter, Section 2.2.3: with a mobile app one selects the type, amount, and mixture of fragrances in dozens of options.

DOES YOUR PURSE LOOK LIKE THIS?

Pouchee[17] (bags to be put inside the purses) will be more **in need** the (1) greater the *number of handbags ladies* on average have, (2) the *frequency* with which they change purses (everyday? once a week?), and (3) the level of *inconvenience* felt when changing items from one bag to another.

Thus the behavioral questions of:

- How many handbags **do you have**?
- How **often** do you **change** handbags?
  Daily?
  Several times a week?
  Once a week?
  Several times a month?
  Never?

- On a 1 (none)–5 (all) scale, what percentage of your purses **have** pockets?
- When changing handbags what is the **average time** you spend replacing items from one into the other?
- On a scale of 1 (do not care)–5 (hate) how do you **feel** about purses without pockets?

When using behavioral interviews to predict future behavior based on past actions, **four** aspects must be taken care of.

First, *who* should participate in the survey?

The answer is: the **target segment**. The type of clients one has in mind, those to whom one wishes to sell.

---

[17]Also an example of the previous chapter, Section 2.2.3.

Many may want the product. But it is better, both in terms of market launch later and the survey test now, to focus on the subset of customers who we believe want the product very, very, very much.

Thus, the more (relevant) variables one uses to define the target client, the better:

- Age?
- Life cycle phase (from young singles to retirees)?
- Genre?
- Social class?
- Ethnicity?
- Political orientation?
- And so on

As long as the above variables are relevant, they pertain to the **marketing plan** to launch the innovation into the market. Although a very important topic, it is outside the PISA scope here, which goes until the *day before* market launch. D-day and afterward is another matter. That will be analyzed in the conclusion.

Second, *how large* should the *sample* size be?

The answer is fourfold: (1) always more than *30*; (2) preferably *100*; (3) never more than *10 percent* of the size of the market target; and (4) a precise answer can be obtained by a sample size *calculator*.

Always more than *30* for statistical reasons: the distribution tends to normal (the mean sample tends to the population mean), thus allowing to use normal statistics such as the confidence level and interval.

Then it is generally believed that the minimum sample size to get a meaningful result is *100* and a maximum not more than *10 percent* of the population.

For a precise answer, there are many available *sample size calculators* online, where one plugs the confidence level one wishes (probability of being true), the range (interval within which the true value is contained), and the population size, and the calculator indicates how many respondents the questionnaire should have.[18]

Third, one of the simplest ways to organize the survey is by using online sites such as Momentive/SurveyMonkey or SurveySparrow, which over 130 countries tap an audience of more than 175 million. Panel members are paid and can be divided by more than 50 attributes such as:

- Hobbies;
- Employment status and type;
- Genre;
- Age;
- Income;
- Number and age of children;
- Health;
- Lifestyle;
- And so on.

And **finally**, how much does it *cost?*

It depends on the site, the number of questions in each questionnaire, how large the sample is (the number of respondents),

---

[18]The sample size depends on (1) what one wants as the confidence interval (the range of plus x percent and minus x percent, which contains the true value: the lower the interval the greater the precision); (2) the confidence level one wishes (the probability that the obtained value is accurate: the larger, the better); and (3) the market size one wants information from (here, the larger the market size, the larger should be the sample, although it does not increase proportionally).

and the type of program opted for: for instance, Momentive/SurveyMonkey charges ± \$380 for 10 answers from 100 participants.

3.5.2. Direct Emotional Assessment

The target of behavioral interviews is actions. Past and present. And through net sample surveys.

DOLLAR SHAVE CLUB

To evaluate emotions, however, **direct emotional assessment** is more adequate.

Here questionnaires are replaced by **direct contact** when talking with friends (the idea for Rent the Runway came from the founder seeing her sister systematically overspend in new dresses for weddings), doing small talk at a party (which led to the Dollar Shave

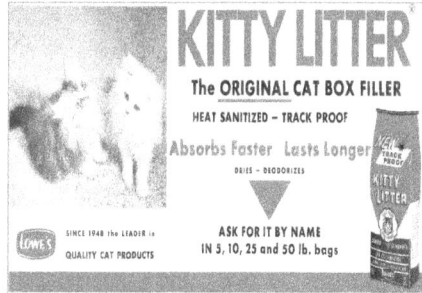

Club innovation described in Chapter 1), or casually bumping into a friend (the idea for Kitty Litter[19] came from Ed Lewis talking with a neighbor).

Indeed any of the above can be the occasion to introduce (softly/ unnoticed to avoid inducing an answer) the **problem** and watch the **reaction**.

In the case of *Ninu* and if having a drink with a friend: you know what? I am using a new perfume but ... I still carry the old one in my purse ... just...

---

[19]Kitty Litter is a construction material clay granulate also used as a sand substitute for cats' boxes, with the advantage of being more absorbent and emitting a pleasant smell.

And then to observe what the reaction is. Is it: really? Which? I know what you mean, it is so hard to decide which and when. The other day…

Or all one gets is a … um … great. Well listen, do you know that I am thinking of buying a new car…?

In the case of *Pouchee*: sorry for being late. I just had to return an important call. And for starts I couldn't find the phone in my purse. They are always such a mess…

And again what's the reaction? Something like: don't get me started. I can't understand why purses are always so messy. The other day…

Or?: … quite … do you know who I met the other day and is starting a new job?

To sum up, **behavioral interviews** assess past (and present) **actions** as the best predictors for the future, While **Direct Emotional Assessment** focuses on **emotions**.

And both together indicate the **potential** of the opportunity.

3.6. Summarizing

The previous chapter identified **opportunities** that literally come to us in the form of **five types of problems**.

The next chapter will analyze how those **problems** can be solved *by adapting solutions already in use elsewhere*, instead of creating them anew from scratch, be they new products or services.

In-between both there is a fundamental question: Does the problem **deserve** a solution? Is it **worthwhile**?

Such a task was decomposed in this chapter into five parts:

> 1st—Does the problem pass the test of **time**?
> 2nd—How to select the **best** (problem/opportunity)?
> 3rd—What is the **job to be done** by the solution in detail?
> 4th—What do customers **at present do** about the problem?
> 5th—How general, **pervasive**, is the problem?

The answers to these five queries make the **difference** between something negligible, nothing more than a small inconvenience to be endured as part of normal daily life, and a real issue, an aggravation, worthwhile investing time, energy, and money into solving it.

And that even if the solution to address the problem will not be constructed anew, but simply **adapted** from another use.

How to do that is the subject of the next chapter, which we will now turn to.

CHAPTER 4

Adapting Solutions That Already Exist (No Need to Create Them)

Knowledge is power; information is power.

Robin Morgan

4.0. Overview

Chapter 2 indicated **opportunities** that come to us in the form of **problems**: (1) *bothers*, (2) *product incompetencies*, (3) *complications*, (4) *concerns*, and (5) *lack of true happiness*.

And *Chapter 3* the **tests** to be performed on the opportunities: (1) *time*, (2) *focus*, (3) *defining well* the problem, (4) isn't there already a *solution* somewhere? and (5) how people *act and react* emotionally to the problem.

It is *now* time to find **solutions** to the problems/opportunities. Most preferably **adapting** solutions already in use elsewhere, rather than constructing them (be it a product or service) anew.

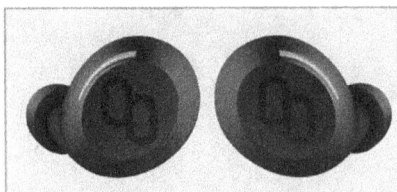

That **minimizes the know-how** needed. Most specifically for highly technically sophisticated products. Such as the *Click Earbuds* that auto-translate into 40 languages: built by a British-Ghanaian entrepreneur it enables communication, text to speech, vice versa and its wireless Bluetooth system can sync with smartphones.

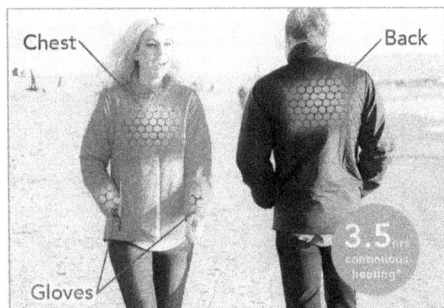

Or *Flexwarm*, the world's smart jacket. A smartphone enables to control the coat's temperature to the accuracy of one degree: integrated into the jacket is an interior and exterior sensor that automatically adjusts the heating level based on the exterior temperature.

And **all around the world** there are other examples of innovations that require extensive know-how.

From **Catalonia** in Spain came *Wallbox*, the home charger for electric vehicles, and Japan offered Spiber, which creates textile materials such as fibers, using biotech fermentation instead of animal or vegetable sources.

Sweden is the birthplace of the unicorn *Klarna*: a net payment processing system for the e-commerce industry, it also offers customer credit on purchases. Handling 35 billion online sales per year and 40 percent of Swedish e-commerce, it is worth $46 billion.

Flyte is the first levitating bulb, a 2015 innovation by the American **Simon Morris** using technology first discovered a century before by the Austrian-Hungarian Nikola Tesla. And this is an example of the *difference* between *invention* (creating a new product) and *innovation* (launching it into the market).

All the above innovations are very useful. But they require extensive know-how that is time consuming to obtain.

Thus we want to the extent possible to stay away from that.

The *question* is: *how*? And the *answer* is that there are **six ways**.

First by using the **internet**. Telephone and fax always enabled many services, including home delivery. But online use enlarges that and opens many other possibilities.

Then it is possible to *adapt solutions* already in use in other **places** (*geographical areas or distribution channels*) or serving other **needs** or type of **clients**.

Still there are many examples of great innovations by simply **adding** or **deducting** (*quantitatively or qualitatively*) one or more accessory characteristic to **existing** products or services.

And **finally** if none of the above is possible, sometimes there is a **patented product** whose inventor had no interest in putting it in the market and therefore is for sale (the example of Flyte is an extreme example where it took 100 years to go from invention to innovation).

Let's turn to these types of solutions.

4.1. Applying the Internet to Products or Services

Regarding previous means of communication (e.g., phone) the **internet** has two advantages: visualization and speed.

Thus it improves some services. And enables others.

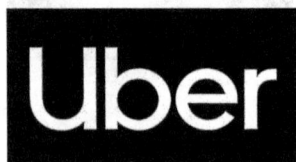

Uber (USA), *Bolt* (Estonia), and *Glovo* (Spain) have been in broad terms expanding from car rentals to e-scooters and bikes, restaurant deliveries, software taxi platforms, supermarket deliveries, and even nonfood deliveries. And they are all unicorns.

Another case is the German *Gorillas*. Founded in 2020 it took only nine months to achieve unicorn status and when operating in 60 cities in nine countries was acquired by Getir in December 2022 for $1.2 billion.

Its business model is simply delivery of supermarket goods in 10 minutes. Operating from dark stores[20] exclusively and with employees using electric bikes, it started with Kagan Sümer buying groceries from local

---

[20]The name given to supermarkets that are not open to the public and thus are indeed simple warehouses.

supermarkets, storing them in his flat, announcing through a mobile app focusing on his neighborhood, and using his own bike.

Four things are interesting here. *First*, Gorillas' business model is not new. Peapod and Home Grocer in the 1990s were the innovators but failed because online use was not as widespread then as it is now. GoPuff followed in 2013 in Philadelphia.[21]

They all "were right," only ahead of time. Now with the universal use of the internet that business model is far more timely.

Second, before the internet the business model existed already, only that it was incipient. One could phone the grocery store at the corner and ask Mr. Williams if he could be kind enough to deliver a basket of products that would then arrive ... as soon as possible.

Third, as Philip Kotler, founder of modern marketing, noted in his memories, the internet is so powerful that it goes far beyond being simply one more channel as it also creates opportunities and (*fourth*) the possibility of changing business models.

An example of new opportunities is *Too Good To Go*, the digital platform referred in Chapter 2, which enables restaurants to sell surplus food (in magic boxes) at a discount to nearby consumers.

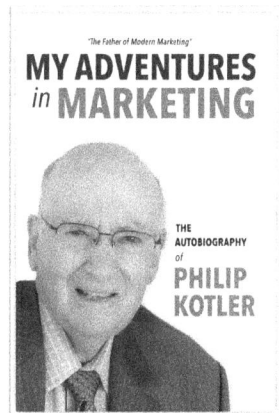

"The Father of Modern Marketing"

MY ADVENTURES
in **MARKETING**

THE AUTOBIOGRAPHY *of*
PHILIP KOTLER

---

[21]As said two and half years after its inception (from May 2020 to December 2022), Gorillas was acquired by its main competitor Getir for 1.2 billion. The reasons for Getir to acquire Gorillas were to (1) increase market share in the European countries where both were present, (2) strengthen the position in others (United States), and (3) access 180 dark stores that were becoming increasingly harder to build due to stringer regulations against noise.

Gorillas needed to sell because it was cash strapped for having grown too fast and demonstrating again how Peter Drucker was so right when he stressed that in entrepreneurship cash is king. Anyway the price was 1.2 billion.

airbnb Another example is Airbnb (shortened version of AirBed and Breakfast) that offers short-term living quarters and breakfast to those unable to book a hotel room in a saturated market. The company acts as a broker with its site linking homeowners with clients and charging a fee for each booking.[22]

Athelas And an illustration of change in business model is given by the unicorn *Athelas*, which having for long sold weight scales, blood pressure monitors, and glucometers, now uses a phone app to convey instant information to nurses and physicians regarding if patients are taking medicaments as prescribed through the use of a box called Pilltrack.

In short, the first type of solution to ponder, before anything else, is the possibility of applying the internet.

If that fails, then let's look what *other places* do about the problem.

4.2. Importing the Solution from Other Places

By other places is meant *two* things: distinct **geographical areas** and different **distribution channels**.[23]

---

[22]The business started when Brian Chesky and Joe Gebbia had the idea of putting an air mattress in their living room and turning that into a bed and breakfast operation.

[23]Still within places there are two other sources both for opportunities and solutions, namely **Nature** and **History**.

However, being much less productive than other *geography* and *distribution channels* they will not be developed here.

Nevertheless, a few examples are worthwhile.

Nature can be divided into: vegetable world, animals, and human physiognomy.

An example of great innovations that came from the **vegetable world** is *Velcro* (junction of the words velvet with crochet) and

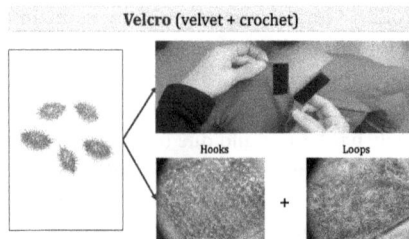

Velcro (velvet + crochet)

Hooks   Loops

+

(continues in the next page)

Most are familiar with two American icons in dolls: *Barbie* and *American Girl.*

What may be less known is that neither was created in the United States but rather both concepts were "imported" from Germany.

---

discovered by Georges de Mestral. He noticed that when walking his dog in the Swiss mountains, there were a few particles that tended to stick both to his clothes and the dog's hair.

Intrigued, a microscope inspection revealed that they were basically constituted by a set of hooks and loops that de Mestral reproduced in tissue, first in cotton and then in nylon and polyester that proved far better. And so Velcro was born.

For those interested in the **animal world**, the book *Smart Swarm* by Peter Miller will make passionate reading, specifically on the lessons by ants. The way they operate has been the inspiration for route optimization in many instances, including *Southwest Airlines* cargo operations and the *Texas division of the French company Air Liquide,* by translating the ant behavior into an algorithm and applying it to decide how trucks should go about their routes among factories and customer's sites. That allowed Air Liquide to save millions of dollars.

On Swarm Intelligence, the *Harvard Business Review* article with the same title by E. Bonabeau and C. Meyer also provides whole new ways to think about business.

Exemplifying how human **physiognomy** can be an inspiration for solutions is *Soundbender,* the plastic magnet that deflects laptop sounds and was discussed in Chapter 2.

Its concave shape replicates what the innovator Moshe Weiss did and people in general do, when they wish to reorient sound: they put the hand in the shape of shells.

History has also been another great source for innovations. The way U.S. mail organized *Pony Express* was a replica of the South American Inca messenger (chasquis) system.

And *vending machines* that today make available all types of products were first introduced in the first century AD to regulate the amount of holy water that temple worshippers received: they would put a coin, a lever would be activated, a valve opened, and a limited amount of holy water dispensed. Hero of Alexandria, a Greek engineer and mathematician, was the innovator.

Thus both **Nature** and **History** are places where the inspiration for solutions can be found. But they are far less productive than (other) *geographical areas* and (other) *distribution channels*, as the main text of the book will show.

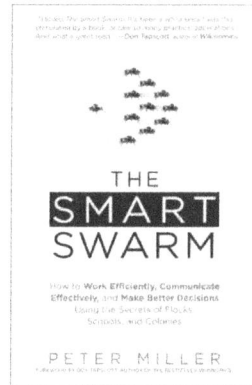

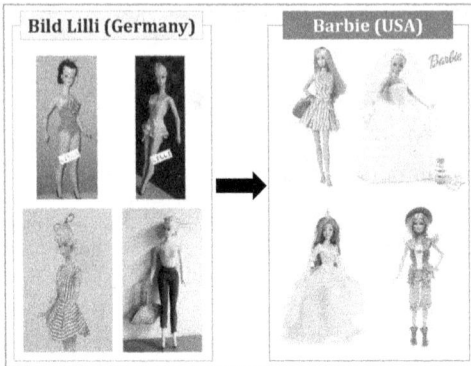

Ruth Handler watched that her daughter Barbara, while playing with paper dolls, gave them adult roles. By contrary, at the time toy dolls were representations of infants.

The prototype to fill that market gap was found by Handler during a family trip to Europe when she saw the German Bild Lilli doll. And so *Barbie* was born.

It was also Germany that inspired *American Girl*: a high-quality pretty doll to play the role of daughters to girls and as an add-up to bring U.S. history alive to them. The role model was a doll manufactured by Götz Puppenfabrik in Rodenthal, Germany.

In the case of Barbie and American Girl, the solution came from a similarly developed country (Germany). But it does not have to be so.

Far less developed countries, such as India, have also been the source of great innovations in the United States, as exemplified by *Fresh Paper*.

When **Kavita Shukla** was spending her holidays with her grandparents in India, she inadvertently swallowed water while washing her teeth.

Fearing that she would become sick, her grandmother gave her a tea with the Indian herb *Fenugreek* used in India for such situations.

Back to the United States Shukla applied the herb to paper for wrapping up food, to make products stay fresh between two and four times longer. And so **Fresh Paper** was born.

As a consequence of prolonging the life of all kinds of food products, whether outdoors or in the freezer, Fresh Paper (followed by some other minor innovations) not only created a $26 million company but also contributes to solving a social problem: keeping products fresh in food banks and helping farmers in the developing world extend the life of their crops once they were picked up (around 25 percent of the world's food supply is lost to spoilage).

While Fresh Paper is a product, developing countries can also be the inspiration for great solutions in the service area, for example, the hub system for airlines to minimize the number of routes.

First invented by the *Indian Post Office*, it was imported to the United States by **Delta Airlines** for passenger travel and finally adapted by **Federal Express** for cargo.

The above examples are imports of ideas between similarly developed countries and from poorer to richer countries. But the reverse can also happen: from richer to poorer countries and even if the innovation is of low price.

Havaianas is one of the few true global brands of Brazil, with over 200 million units sold yearly in more than 100 countries. And thus a unicorn.

Afonso Oliveira and **Robert Fraser** found a solution to Brazil's extensive number of poor people going barefoot, with a very low-priced open shoe given the warm weather.

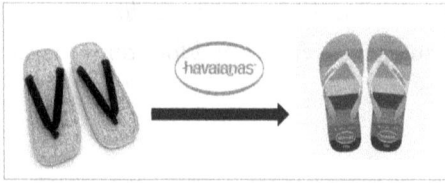

The search led them to adapt *Zori*, the Japanese sandals made of hay and wood, into rubber in the case of Brazil. Initially sold only to the poorer classes it became later a trendy brand used by all social classes all over the world (the U.S. price ranges from $11 to $75).

That geography is indeed a rich source of solutions is exemplified still by Bear Hostels, the highly successful Russian chain of hostels: an idea imported from Germany, when Daniil Mishin, having missed his flight, had to stay overnight in Berlin.

And Madeira Madeira is a Brazilian 2009 "clone" of the 2001 U.S. Bizchair.com: a virtual furniture store.

Thus when the internet (as seen in the previous section) fails, it is worthwhile to look around the **whole** globe scrutinizing what people do about the problem. Regardless of a country's stage of development, ahead, similar or worse, than ours.

There is another subaspect of place, besides geography, that can generate solutions: *distribution channels*.

To minimize the time spent in getting laundry done, it's best to locate the solution in the path from and to people's work. That is what *Click n' Clean* did with placing lockers in parking lots and building halls, with the service being paid for online.

Another example is *L'eggs*, hosiery for the over 40-year-old working women of middle-low social classes ($C_1 + C_2$).

The question is how to get to them, the target clients, if they hardly have time to go into department stores, shopping malls, or specialized stores?

Since many novelties in groceries are brought to attention by stand-alones in between the stands and cashiers, supermarket booths were the solution adopted by L'eggs.

In short, **place** (other *geographies* and different *distribution channels*) together with applying the internet are relatively simple and pervasive solutions. But what if none of them work?

Then it may be useful to look at how *other* **types of clients** satisfy a similar need.

4.3. Importing the Solution from Other Clients

That is quite a productive source, regardless of what the solution is for: simple leisure; daily life; or high-risk activities.

Many when enjoying long walks with their dog bring beverages for hydration. But what about the dog? Bottles are not practical and natural sources are not always available.

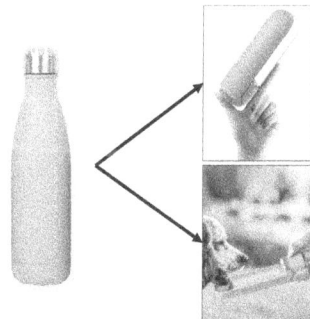

The solution is *Redminut*, a simple adaptation of the thermos bottle for our best friends.

High or medium-heeled shoes are elegant and a must for many events. But a source of ache. How to alleviate the pain as soon as one is on the way home?

Ballet dancers   Funk-tional

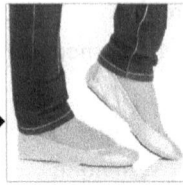

Funk-tional provided the solution by adapting it from ballet dancers' shoes. They are very light and flexible footwear so that they can be folded and kept within a purse and when needed taken out to replace the high-heeled shoes.

According to the World Health Organization, nearly 1.5 million people lose their lives in road accidents each year. Half of the accidents are caused by mobile phones whose use is especially dangerous when driving motor bikes.

What do other types of clients (e.g., aircraft pilots) do about the problem? To communicate, use GPS and control other information? They have technology inbuilt into their helmets.

So why not adapt that to the motor bikers' helmets?

That is what **Romain Duflot**, the founder of *Eyelights* and both a motorbike enthusiast and a trained fighter pilot, did (creating a net worth company of ± $150 million).

So, the solution used to satisfy other clients can frequently be adapted to our problem and our client: from humans to dogs; from ballet dancers to ladies using high-heeled shoes; and from aircraft pilots to motor bikers. But what if nothing of the sort is to be found?[24]

---

[24]Other clients is a powerful source, not only of solutions but also of opportunities, as exemplified by the unicorn *Fenty Beauty*.

Promoted as an all-inclusive make-up for all types of skins, from lightest to darkest, most of its ads focus on women of color with deeper skin tones. The type of client is the novelty (opportunity). And not the product (shade/make-up) or the need (give color, hide imperfections, and improve appearance).

4.4. Adapting the Solution from Other Needs

When facing an unsatisfied need (and thus an opportunity), the question to be asked is: what is done regarding similar needs? What are the solutions there? And then, adapt them.

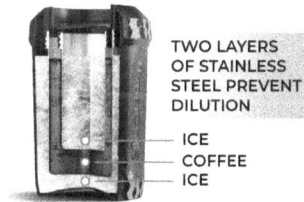

The stream of such innovation is numerous. *Crayon holders* (invented by the 12-year-old Cassidy Goldstein) prevents wax pencils from breaking using basically the same type of glass tubes utilized to hold the flowers' calluses.

The **thermos** bottle used to maintain a beverage temperature was the inspiration of the *Ice Cream Canteen* that freezes an ice cream for four hours.

TWO LAYERS OF STAINLESS STEEL PREVENT DILUTION
ICE
COFFEE
ICE

The **cocktail shaker** was the source for the *HyperChiller* Iced Coffee, a plastic bottle that makes frozen coffee in one minute.

Lola Rola replaces vacuum cleaners with the advantages of being far lighter, less expensive, less noisy, and (for being smaller) easier to fit below maples, chairs, and furniture.

It removes all types of dirt including pet's hair with ... paper embedded glue. Just like **scotch tape** and **glue rolls** to clean clothes.

When doing the laundry an important time saving step is to keep socks together to avoid having to pair them afterward, as well as their eventual disappearance into pockets and the insides of others' clothes.

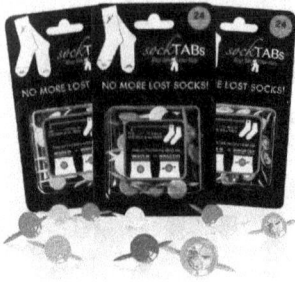

Keeping things together, while being easy to separate when one wishes, is what **clips** and **pins** do. And so was born *SockTabs*, made of plastic, to avoid damaging the socks and creating rust in the laundry machine.

Sales are $200,000 a year and profits high: production cost $1.25; retailer cost $4.99; consumer price $9.99. Company value: $1 million.

Readerest is basically **two magnets** to hold glasses in the shirt (one magnet in the inside and the other on the outside of the shirt). An idea that did 13 million in sales in the three years following the initial air date. At present it makes $5 million a year on sales.

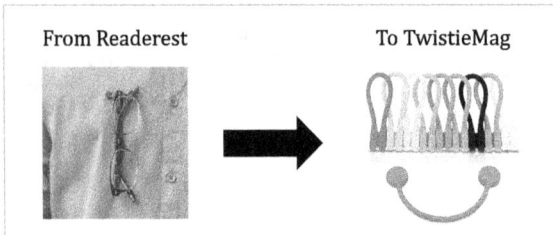

And *TwistieMag* is a simple **adaptation of Readerest** for many other purposes: sticking the ear phone wire to the gym shirt, closing the cereal bags, sticking messages in the fridge, bundling computer cables, and so on.

The above examples give a simple message: when facing an unsatisfied need, it is frequently useful to ask how are similar needs being satisfied?

But what if there is no satisfactory answer?

Then, there is still the alternative of looking at the closest available product and acting upon it.

Take an **old product** item and	Add	Deduct
Quantitatively (palpable, tangible)	1	3
Qualitatively	2	4

Figure 10 Changing a product by acting upon accessory characteristics

4.5. Adding or Deducting Slight Changes in the Product

By slight, minor alterations is meant maintaining the product **core** and adding or deducting, quantitatively or qualitatively, **accessory** characteristics (Figure 10).

Adding quantitatively (cell one), represents two (or more) in one.

As air travel intensifies, airports are becoming ever larger. As carrying bags may not be a problem as they (now)[25] have wheels, the required long walking on never-ending corridors yes. At least for some.

Thus came the solution of adding a scooter to the hand baggage (*Olaf Kick Scooter*). The baggage does not have to be dispatched. The wheels prevent the baggage from being cumbersome. And the scooter from having to walk long distances.

---

[25]An innovation by Travelpro.

The same principle has been used by *Roller Buggy* (baby strollers with a scooter), *TernX Carry-On* (a hybrid on luggage and stroller), and the *StashAll* line of

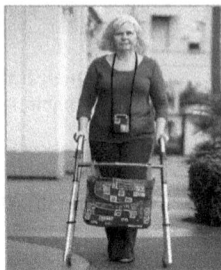

bags: when older ladies need a walker, carrying a handbag becomes difficult. The solution is walkers that allow for bags to be hung upon.

Other times, the addition rather than *quantitative* can be **qualitative**, when the addition is **intangible**.

That is the case with *BB Cream*, which is five in one: moisturizer, skin treatment, concealer, foundation, and sunscreen. A success promptly imitated by brands such as Garnier, Vichy, and Nivea.

Knix, period underwear, is another example. Being super leakproof it absorbs between 6 and 20 tampons of blood (depending on the style), thus making unnecessary the pads and tampons on top of underwear and the enjoyment of worry-free protection from blood and all other forms of liquids (sweats and so on). Knix, invented by **Joanna Griffiths**, solves two problems: complications and concerns. And consequently, in a decade became worth half a billion.

Deducting quantitatively is another source of solutions.

Bicycling is a good exercise. But not always allowed either by the weather or where one lives. Thus the *home bicycle* was born by simply **removing** the wheels from a normal bicycle, while keeping everything else: the handlebar, the frame, the pedals, the gear, the seat. Everything is kept, only the wheels are removed.

Babies' chairs started with basic seats with the legs removed, and hands-free umbrellas to play golf, go fishing, and so on are the result of simply removing the stems.

Also the unicorn Spanx, described in the introduction, is a normal pantyhose **cut** by the length of the leg.

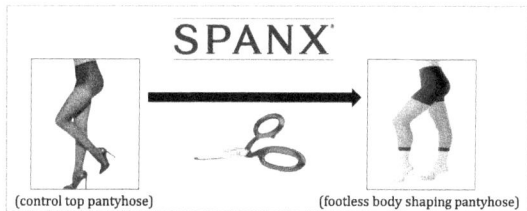

SPANX

(control top pantyhose)   (footless body shaping pantyhose)

Finally, **deduction** can be **qualitative** (not quantitative), as the hugely successful *QB House* and *Fast Eddies* barber shop chains exemplify.

Launched in different parts of the world, their principle is the same: faster (and thus cheaper) haircuts, by eliminating hair wash (replaced in both cases by using a small vacuum cleaner) and

also in the instance of the Japanese *QB House* by dispensing the traditional Japanese hot towels, shoulder massages, tea and skin treatment. QB House's clients in seven years went from 57,000 to three and half million.

4.6. The Last Solution: Buying Patents

What if all previous sources of solutions **fail**? The **internet**. Importing from other **geographical areas**. And from distinct **distribution channels**. Adapting from different **clients**. Or **needs**. **Adding** quantitatively to the product. Adding qualitatively. **Decreasing** in quantity. Or in quality.

What if nothing of the above works? Then, before creating a new product or a service from scratch, there is still the possibility that a **patent** on a gadget that solves the problem is available for sale.

That is what **Rick Hopper**, the inventor of *Readerest* (the magnet glasses holder)[26] did.

Having developed the idea on his own, he discovered, when applying for the patent, that it had already been filled in, but the product had not been launched in the market. Again, that exemplifies the difference between an inventor (who creates a new product or service) and an innovator (who launches it into the market). The latter requires a marketing plan, financing, organizing operations, and hiring a team.

Not all inventors are innovators. Many are happy to just invent, patent the gadget, and move on to their next idea while waiting for someone to come up to buy what they have patented.

An extreme case is *Flyte* (the levitator lamp mentioned at the beginning of this chapter), which took one century between the creation of technology and its use.

But there are many others. The patent for the *Bic* pen was filled in by Hungarian inventor **László Bíró**. Both in France and in the United States.

Then the French **Marcel Bich**, who had been working on the very same idea of ballpoint pens for some time, bought the patents from **Bíró** and

---

[26]As mentioned before it works by simply putting a magnet inside and the other outside a shirt, pullover, and such.

using Swiss machine tools founded Bic, a shortened and far easier to re-member version of his own name.

Morgan invented the first traffic control device with three signals: stop, caution, and go. And it was hand operated. **General Electric**, which had been working on an electric version of the signal, bought the patent from Morgan and went to monopolize the manufacturing of traffic signals in the whole of the United States.

Throughout history women have been soaking up their periods with all sorts of devices: tissue, rags, sponges, and even paper and moss.

The first tampon with an applicator was invented by **Earle Haas** con-sisting of a cotton plug and two pieces of cardboard. Haas named the patent *Tampax*.

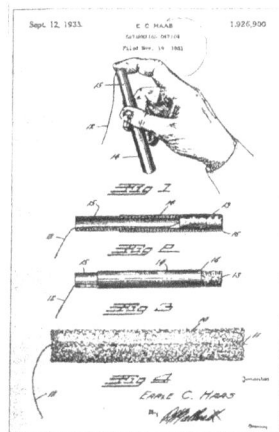

Lacking marketing skills, Haas' involvement with Tampax ended in the very same year he received the patent by selling it to Gertrude Tendrich.

Inventors and innovators have **different personality characteristics**. And a totally distinct starting point: the *inventor* usually starts with *technology*. The *innovator* with a *problem* to be solved.

That is why the patent for the magnetic eyeglass holder was for sale. And why Rick Hopper bought it and made a huge success out of it.

In conclusion if everything else fails, before creating a solution from scratch, it's advisable to check what is available for sale in terms of patents.

4.7. Synthesis

Sometimes there is no alternative but to solve a problem with a technically sophisticated product (or service) that requires considerable know-how.

Two recent types of pens are such cases: *Tactiv,* which writes underwater and at extreme temperatures (from $-30°F$ to $+250°F$), and *Frixion,* an ink pen that comes with an eraser on top.

If high know-how is the only way, so be it.

But to go straight into such a difficult solution may be a waste of time, energy, and money, if one of the **six** alternatives listed in **Figure 11** solves the problem. So they can and should be tried beforehand, since simplicity is complexity solved.

Is there a **patent** for sale? As the examples of Readerest, Flyte, Bic, traffic signals, and Tampax indicate, not all patented products and technologies are launched into the market.

Even if the patented gadget solves only part of the problem it becomes nevertheless an easier solution to **add** or **deduct** to it the remaining required characteristics.

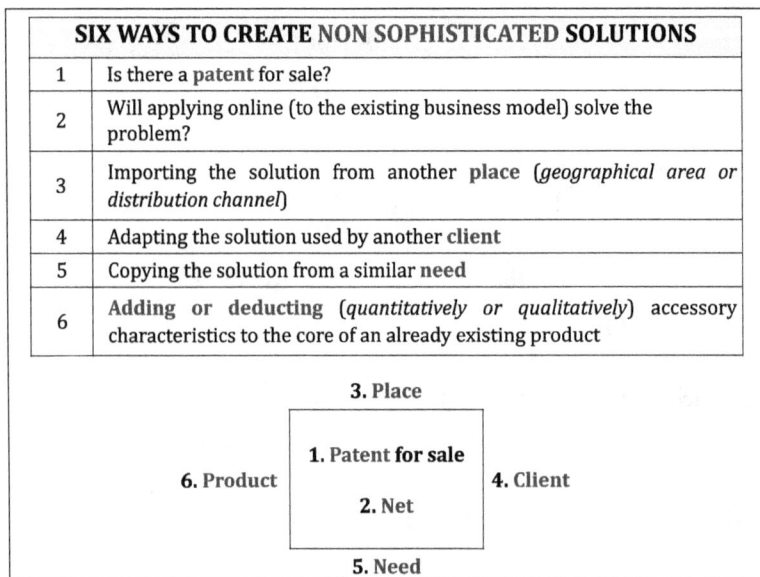

SIX WAYS TO CREATE NON SOPHISTICATED SOLUTIONS	
1	Is there a **patent** for sale?
2	Will applying online (to the existing business model) solve the problem?
3	Importing the solution from another **place** (*geographical area or distribution channel*)
4	Adapting the solution used by another **client**
5	Copying the solution from a similar **need**
6	**Adding** or **deducting** (*quantitatively or qualitatively*) accessory characteristics to the core of an already existing product

3. Place

6. Product | **1. Patent for sale** | **4. Client**

2. Net

5. Need

Figure 11

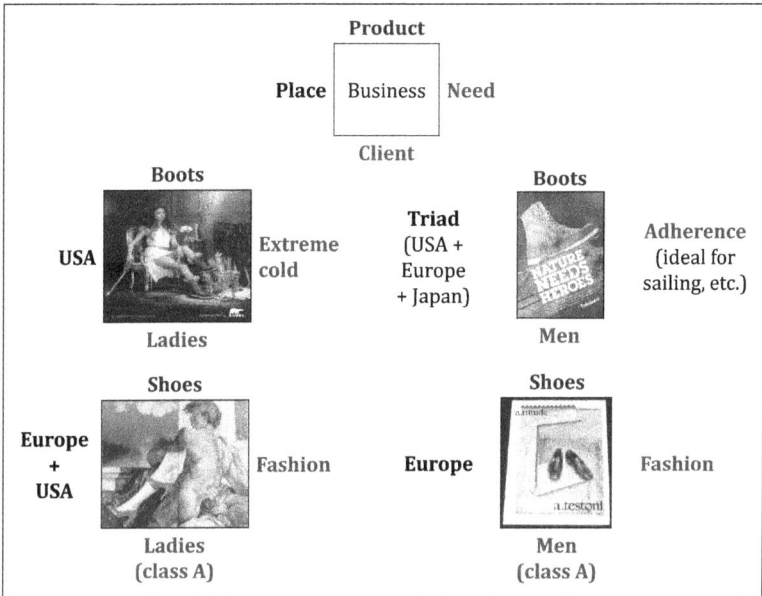

Figure 12 The four sides of a market segment

Then, there is always the possibility of applying the **internet**, as illustrated by Gorillas in distribution (together with Bolt, Glovo, and Uber), Athelas in home care (a unicorn as well), and Too Good To Go (in restaurants).

If neither a **patent** is available nor the **internet** solves the problem, there are still **four** remaining options corresponding to the sides of the square at the bottom of Figure 12: product, place, need, client.

A **market segment** is a (1) *product* satisfying a (2) *client* and a (3) *need* in a given (4) *place*. Thus and as per Figure 12 one can have boots for ladies to be used in extreme cold in the United States (as in the case of the brand Sorels); boots for men providing high adherence (important for sailing and other sports) in the triad (United States, Europe, and Japan)— brand: Timberland; fashionable shoes for class A ladies in Europe and the United States (the brand here is Charles Jordan); or fashionable shoes but now for men (class A) in Europe: Testoni brand.

And so, **the source for a solution can be any side of the square.**

Places: sometimes the solution already exists in other countries (as illustrated by the cases of Delta,[27] Federal Express, Fresh Paper, Havaianas, Barbie, or American Girl) or distinct distribution channels (Click n' Clean and L'eggs).

Other times, **different clients** are already using products that can be adapted to our purposes (Redminut, Funk-tional, Eyelights, Fenty Beauty).

There is still the possibility of directly importing products/services from **similar needs**: Ice Cream Canteen, HyperChiller, Crayon Holders, Lola Rola, SockTabs, Readerest, TwistieMag.

And if everything above fails, then the solution can come from taking an already existing product and **adding or deducting** some accessory characteristics to it: Olaf Kick Scooter, Roller Buggy, Stash all, TernX, BB Cream, Knix, QB House, Fast Eddies, and Spanx are a few of the examples the chapter went over.

In short, any of the above **six sources of solutions** in Figure 11 are alternatives to create solutions from scratch.

And where does that leave us? Chapter 2 analyzed how *problems are opportunities in disguise*. Chapter 3 how to *test* their importance. And *this chapter* exploited *simple alternatives* to create a solution anew.

What is left? The next step: **Action**, which is the subject of the **following chapter**.

---

[27]Examples used in this chapter.

CHAPTER 5

Action (Decisive and Nonexpensive)

Action is the greatest eloquence.

Shakespeare

5.0. Overview

The previous chapters:

1. Identified a **problem** that constitutes an opportunity;
2. Tested it for **frequency**; and
3. **Relevance**;
4. Then selected the single most pressing opportunity to enable **focus**;
5. Next the **problem characteristics** that the solution must address were defined in detail;
6. One confirmed that nowhere in the market there is an alternative **solution**; as well as that
7. Many people **feel** deeply about the problem; and finally:
8. A solution was **adapted** from somewhere else (preferable to creating a new one).

Thus, it is now time for **action**: for *launching the product into the market.*

That requires the following steps:

> *First*: a **prototype** to be built;
> *Second*: a **patent** request initiated (the emphasis here is in *beginning* the process and keeping it *alive*) together with **trademarking** the name, logo, and slogan;
> *Third*: a **focus group** used (for improvements on the prototype); and
> *Fourth*: a **gradual** market launch (to minimize cost and risk).

Those are the next sections.[28]

5.1. Prototype

The word comes from the **Greek** Protos (first) and Typos (type), that is, a first model, be it of a garment, electric device, toy, or shoe. Whatever.

---

[28]As has been said, action is the greatest eloquence. Many entrepreneurs struggle with implementing their ideas. So this chapter is designed **both** to be (1) **skimmed** by those wishing only a general knowledge or (2) used as a **detailed manual/vademecum** for those wanting to launch their inventions into the market.

It involves the **three** basic phases of (1) a *drawing* (by hand or using CAD—Computer-Aided Design); (2) a *mold* (the cast, the case); and (3) the *material* that will be placed within.

A few aspects are noteworthy. **First**, all those involved in making a prototype must sign a *nondisclosure agreement*. **Second**, there are prototypes for both *products and services*. In the latter case they may be *storyboards* (visual presentations illustrating a sequence of events and interactions) or *role-playing* (simulations with actors playing out different roles).

Third, the *cost* of doing a prototype varies and financing can be obtained through crowdfunding platforms such as Kickstarter, which was used, for example, by Moshe Weiss, the inventor of Soundbender (the sound deflector for laptops).[29]

Fourth, so that the prototypes be worthwhile, they must be an accurate representation of the innovation, therefore made in considerable *detail*. For instance *Visivox*, the invention of Doris Drucker (wife of the great Peter Drucker, founder of modern management), is a device to indicate speakers when they have to raise their voice to be heard at the very end of an auditorium. Prototype details involved deciding on the size of the box, material it would be made of (plastic or metal?), number of microphones (she decided on two, one in the box and the other outside linked to a cable so that the speaker could move around), the number of internal circuits, the color of the warning lights, a strap to carry the box around, and so on.

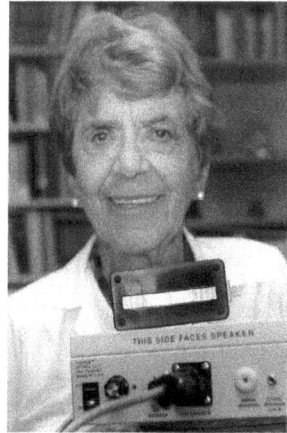

However, **details** are as important as dangerous since they can be a **trap**: the inventor goes on and on and on, in a never-ending process leading to procrastinating and delaying forever market entry.

[29]Referred in Section 4.4, Chapter 4.

And so a balance must be attained between accuracy and perfectionism (that Churchill said should be spelled ... paralysis).

In order to know when the prototype is ready and thus one should stop improving it, there are **two** rules.

First, to keep in mind what the prototype is for: (1) facilitating obtaining a *patent*, (2) working with a *focus group*, and (3) a gradual launch into the market through getting orders in *fairs and shows*.

The **second** rule is to look at the prototype and see when improvements stop compensating the ever smaller number of imperfections. Salespeople and sales reps are not buying our innovation for its perfection, but for its **novelty**. As long as the latter is strong they are willing to accept imperfections in the first models. They understand that that is part of an evolving process. As has been said, the way is made as one moves along.

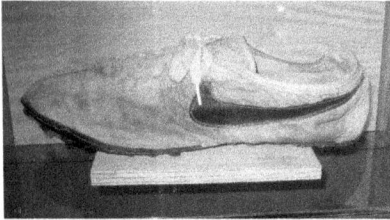

Nike, at its early stages, launched the "Moon Shoe" at the 1972 Chicago National Sporting Goods Association show. The model had still many flaws: the leather was shiny not in a good way; the logo was crooked; the upper, coated with polyurethane, had several defects.

However, by the end of the first day, orders exceeded Nike's founder Phil Knight's grandest expectations and Nike was one of the smash hits of the show.

In spite of being flawed, sales reps loved the shoes. The upper part of the shoe and the outer sole were made of the spongy surface polyurethane and with the design of a waffle iron.

The name Nike came from Athena Nike, the **Greek goddess of victory**. The logo: what's this? asked a sales rep to Phil Knight; it's a **swoosh**, the sound of someone going past you. They even loved the color of the shoe boxes: bright neon orange, the boldest color in the rainbow.

The point is to stop improving the prototype when the flaws become insignificant regarding the novelty the good already brings. Not when there are no flaws.

Anyway, **prototypes are a must** for one or more of **four** reasons.

To discuss the idea with *focus groups*: when **Rowland** introduced the concept of the *American Girl doll* to a group of mothers and grandmothers, for the first 45 minutes they hated it; when she finally presented the prototype to them … they loved it.

As an *image* is worth a thousand words, people learn more by the eyes than by the ears.[30] Thus it also *facilitates the patent* process, enhancing what's unique about the innovation.

And finally, a prototype is fundamental to get *first orders* in shows and fairs without going immediately into large-scale manufacturing. Besides being of course a must to *guide* factories into production.

And from here **three** questions follow: who *can* make a prototype? Who *best* to do it? And *how to go* about it?

Two stories illustrate best the answer to these questions: *Baby Toon* and *Nike*. Baby Toon because of the age of the entrepreneur. And Nike as it was one step from bankruptcy for lack of cash.

---

[30]Father Antonio Vieira, a Portuguese Jesuit of the late 16th and 17th centuries.

Baby Toon is a riskless spoon for babies, created by **Cassidy Crowley** who was tired of seeing her mother's worries with the newborn Cassidy's sister who loved, as babies do, to put everything in her mouth. The sharp edge of spoons presented a risk, but not the animal-shaped toys made of silicone.

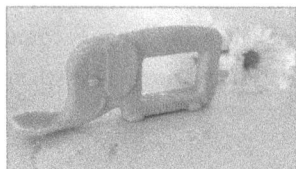

So, why not make a spoon out of silicone, in the shape of toys, for example, an elephant, without any sharp edges and the spoon not too deep? A spoon equal to a toy. A clone.

The point is that Cassidy was **seven years old** when she made the silicone prototype as part of her first group project in school and soon later was in the market with the company worth $1 million.

Nike is a different but also revealing story. One of its cofounders was **Bill Bowerman**, a 60-year-old athletics coach.

A wealthy alumni of Oregon State University had just donated $1 million for the world's finest racing track of polyurethane, a spongy surface, later to be used in the 1972 Olympics.

However, runners weren't getting the full benefit of the new surface since shoes weren't still gripping at it right.

One Sunday, sitting for breakfast with his wife, Bowerman's gaze drifted to her waffle iron, noticing the waffle iron's gridded pattern.

Having urethane in his garage left over from the installation of the track, he carried the waffle iron out to the garage, filled it with urethane, heated it up, and immediately ruined it: the urethane sealed it shut as Bowerman hadn't added a chemical releasing agent (Bowerman didn't know anything about chemical releasing agents).

So he bought another waffle iron, and this time filled it with plaster, and when the plaster hardened, the jaws of the waffle iron opened. He took the mold to the Oregon Rubber Company to pour liquid rubber into it.

Another failure as the rubber mold being too rigid, too brittle, it promptly broke.

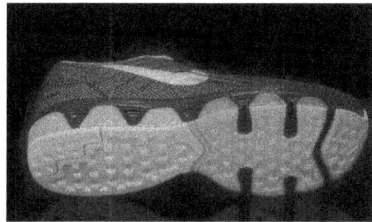

Bowerman went for a third try. Giving up the waffle iron altogether, he took a sheet of stainless steel and punched it with holes, creating a wafflelike surface, and brought that back again to the rubber company. The mold was now pliable, workable to be sewed to the sole of a pair of running shoes. Bowerman gave these to one of his runners and he ran like a rabbit.

Figure 13 summarizes the *differences* and *similarities* in both cases, Baby Toon and Nike.

The *first* difference is in **age**: seven years old in the case of Cassidy Crowley of Baby Toon and the 60 years of Bill Bowerman of Nike. Age does not matter: Lisa Gable of L.G. Accessories was aged 70 when she made her first prototype. And Doris Drucker 82 years old when she launched Visivox.

The *second* difference was the **materials** used. Silicon in Baby Toon and liquid rubber plus stainless steel punched with holes in the outer sole of Nike. And there are many other frequently used materials in molding such as wax, plasticine, clay.

Prototypes / Characteristics	Baby Toon	Nike
Age	7	60
Materials	Silicone	Liquid rubber + stainless steel punched with hole
Third-party intervention?	No	Yes: rubber factory
The **initial and final materials** were the	Same (silicone)	Different (urethane, plaster, liquid rubber)
Clear objective	A funny toy to be used as a harmless spoon	Outer sole with grip but pliable
Detailed requirements	No sharp edges Soft Spoon not deep Easy to grab Funny Different animals and colors	Grip but not gluey Pliable but not too brittle
Absence of know-how	None had any	
Imported from another product	Toy	Waffle iron

Figure 13 Prototype differences and similarities

The *third* difference is that the seven-year-old Cassidy did the prototype **by herself** while Bowerman **hired a factory** to pour liquid rubber in the outer sole he had made.

And *fourth*, in the case of Baby Toon the **material** of the first and final version of the prototype was the **same** (silicone), while **different** in the case of Nike.

Then come the **similarities**. *First* and foremost, in both instances the **objective** was clear, that is, the characteristics of the *job to get done*: a (funny) toy that could be used as (a harmless) spoon and an outer sole with grip but pliable.

Thus, regardless if the prototype is done with the help of a third party or not, for example, a factory, in both instances the *detailed requirements* must come from the entrepreneur, while the prototype is going over several versions.

Two final common aspects are noteworthy: none of the entrepreneurs had considerable *expertise* or **know-how**: one was a first-grade student and the other an athletics coach (not a chemical engineer).

And the idea for the prototype (the solution) came from *importing it* from **other needs**: from toys and a waffle iron.

Among the items summarized in Figure 13 (the first four characteristics are the **differences** and the last four the **similarities**), it is worthwhile to go over briefly how to do molds.

5.1.1. Making Prototypes

The starting point is the overall objective and then one deducts the specific requirements needed to get the job done.

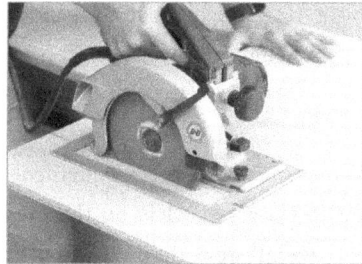

For example, for a *circular saw*[31] the desired outcomes are (by order of importance):

- Minimizing the likelihood that debris will fly up in the air when guiding the blade along the cut line, for example, into the user's face or eyes;
- Decreasing the likelihood of inadvertently moving off the cut line/path when the cut path/line gets covered with dust;
- Diminishing the time it takes to set the angle of the blade, for example, make a bevel adjustment;

---

[31]From *Jobs To Be Done* by A. W. Ulwick; Idea Bite Press; 2016.

- Minimizing the likelihood of snagging the cord on the material when making a long cut;
- Decreasing the time it takes to place the saw back in service when the power cord is cut;
- Diminishing the likelihood that the cut goes off track when finishing the cut;
- Saving the time it takes to secure the saw from falling when it is not in use, for example, from a ladder or rafter;
- Decreasing the likelihood of dropping the saw when lowering it from a ladder/roof.

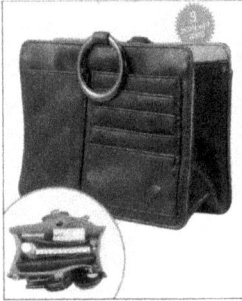

Or in the case of *Pouchee* (the bag to be inserted in all handbags to avoid the need of transferring items among them):

- Size:
  ○ Large enough to contain all items and leaving no voids between the outer and inner bag; but
  ○ Small as needed to fit within most handbags;
- Flexible tissue to adapt to multiple handbag shapes;
- High number of pockets to organize items; and
- Design so that it can be used as a handbag on its own.

When specifying the requirements, in order to avoid a long list it is useful to (1) focus solely on the **most important** and (2) to keep in mind the **overall goal** they are for. Otherwise one becomes lost in details. As *Seneca*, the Roman philosopher and statesman once said, *there are no propitious winds when one does not know where one wants to go.*

Next come **three** phases:

First: Drawing by hand or CAD—Computer-Aided Design;
Second: Making the *mold*, also called the case, the outside shape of the prototype;

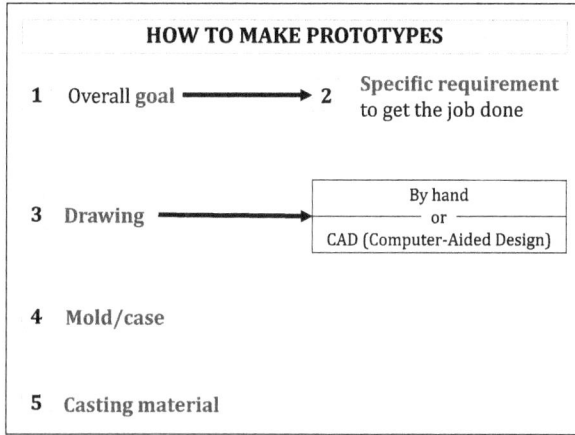

HOW TO MAKE PROTOTYPES

1   Overall goal ⟶ 2   **Specific requirement**
                          to get the job done

3   Drawing ⟶ By hand
                 — or —
                 CAD (Computer-Aided Design)

4   Mold/case

5   Casting material

Figure 14

Although many materials are used to make molds, from paper and cardboard, to foam, plastic, resins, wood, various metals, the most frequent are silicone, latex, alginate, plaster, and clay for being made of rigid materials, but nevertheless workable. And they have different properties as summarized in **Figure 15**.

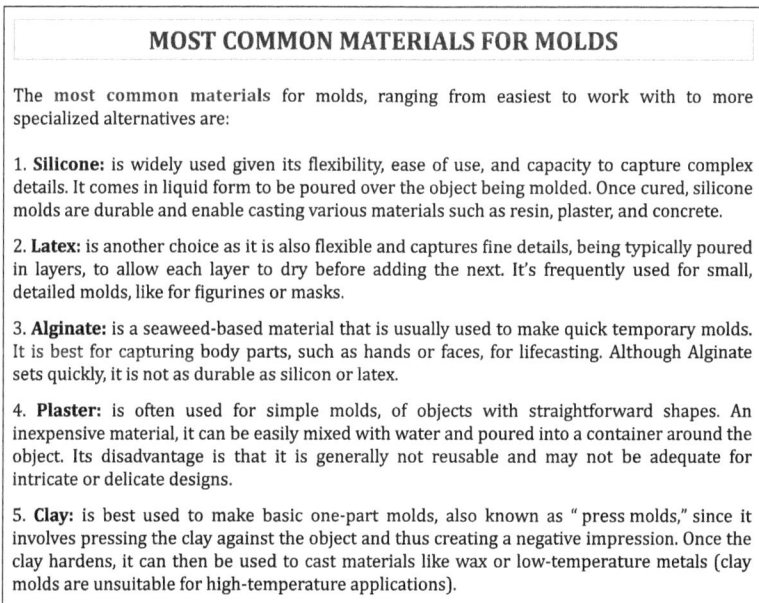

MOST COMMON MATERIALS FOR MOLDS

The most common materials for molds, ranging from easiest to work with to more specialized alternatives are:

1. **Silicone:** is widely used given its flexibility, ease of use, and capacity to capture complex details. It comes in liquid form to be poured over the object being molded. Once cured, silicone molds are durable and enable casting various materials such as resin, plaster, and concrete.

2. **Latex:** is another choice as it is also flexible and captures fine details, being typically poured in layers, to allow each layer to dry before adding the next. It's frequently used for small, detailed molds, like for figurines or masks.

3. **Alginate:** is a seaweed-based material that is usually used to make quick temporary molds. It is best for capturing body parts, such as hands or faces, for lifecasting. Although Alginate sets quickly, it is not as durable as silicon or latex.

4. **Plaster:** is often used for simple molds, of objects with straightforward shapes. An inexpensive material, it can be easily mixed with water and poured into a container around the object. Its disadvantage is that it is generally not reusable and may not be adequate for intricate or delicate designs.

5. **Clay:** is best used to make basic one-part molds, also known as "press molds," since it involves pressing the clay against the object and thus creating a negative impression. Once the clay hardens, it can then be used to cast materials like wax or low-temperature metals (clay molds are unsuitable for high-temperature applications).

Figure 15

And the choice of material depends on factors such as the complexity of the object being molded, the desired level of detail, and the casting material planned to be used.

The **last phase** of a prototype is the *casting*, that is, pouring a liquid material into a mold and allowing it to solidify to obtain the desired shape as the mold contains a cavity that represents the shape of the final object.

Depending on the specific application and requirements, there are several casting materials and mold types used for casting. The most frequent are various types of metal, plastic, and other materials as summarized in **Figure 16**.

And here again the **selection** of *casting material* as well as of the *mold* depends upon the (1) prototype complexity, (2) size, and (3) material properties required.

Regardless of the materials used, the most frequent question on prototypes is, **can one do it all by oneself?**

MOST FREQUENT CASTING MATERIALS

1. **Metal Casting:**
   - Sand Casting: Molten metal poured into a mold of compacted sand;
   - Investment Casting: A wax pattern is coated with a ceramic shell, and the wax is then melted out before pouring the metal into the shell;
   - Die Casting: Under high pressure molten metal is injected into the metal mold;

2. **Plastic Casting:**
   - Injection Molding: High-pressure molten plastic is injected into a mold cavity;
   - Rotational Molding: Plastic powder is first placed in a mold, rotated, and then heated to evenly adapt to and thus coat the mold's interior;
   - Blow Molding: Air pressure expands molten plastic within a mold cavity;

3. **Other Casting Materials:**
   - Concrete Casting: Liquid concrete is poured into a mold to form solid structures;
   - Resin Casting: Liquid resin, commonly mixed with a catalyst, is poured into a mold and allowed to cure to create plastic-like objects;
   - Silicone Casting: Liquid silicone poured into a mold creates flexible and accurate replicas.

Figure 16

The answer is frequently **yes**. After all Cassidy Crowley was **seven** years old when she did her $1 million prototype as a first-grade assignment. Many materials are easy to work with. Many innovations are simple. And solutions frequently are nothing but imported or adapted from other countries, clients, needs, or distribution channels.

That together with the existence of several helpful **sites**[32] is the reason why frequently entrepreneurs without previous knowledge of the field are able to make the prototypes: Lisa Gable of L.G. Accessories, Anita Crook of Pouchee, and Mary Tennyson of StashAll are such examples.

And even when in some instances the prototypes are highly sophisticated the entrepreneur is up to the task: either because he has **know-how** (e.g., Jim Butenschoen of the Career Academy of Hair Design and Gary Burrell, the inventor of GPS); or she **teams up** with who has the required knowledge (Doris Drucker with Visivox partnered with an engineer).

Finally the entrepreneur can also get the *help of* **third-party sources** such as *labs* and *factories* to complete concrete aspects of the prototype (e.g., Bill Bowerman of Nike and Angie Higa of Sky Dreams).[33]

Whatever. The important point is that with a better or worse prototype in hand, one can move into the next phase: filing for **trademarks** and **patents**.

---

[32]For instance: ChatGPT; Wikihow: www.wikihow.com; Autodesk Instructables: www.instructables.com; Formlabs: www.formlabs.com.

[33]In such instances all those involved in making a prototype should sign a non-disclosure agreement.

5.2. Trademarks of Names, Logos and Slogans, and Patents

As they involve different processes it is useful to distinguish between trademarks of *names, logos, and slogans* on one side; and *patents* on the other.

5.2.1. Trademarking Names, Logos and Slogans

What's in a name? A great deal. When Ray Kroc bought the company from the McDonald's brothers who operated a single restaurant in San Bernardino, he also acquired the name.

The brothers kept operating the original restaurant now renamed "The Big M" while Ray Kroc opened a McDonald's across the street.

Although the brothers consistently advertised that they had been in the same location, place, selling hamburgers for over 15 years, and they were thus very well known by the community, clients kept crossing the street to go to McDonald's!..., forcing the brothers to throw in the towel and close The Big M. Meanwhile the McDonald's restaurant boomed…

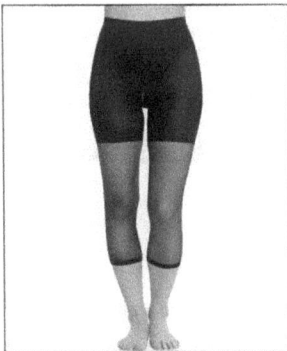

Important as a name is, it must be **registered (trademarked)** for *protection*, which is not too expensive and can be done by anyone: Sara Blakely, the creator of *Spanx* (the footless body shaping pantyhose), trademarked the name Spanx directly in the patent's office website with $150 from her debit card.

At present the (administrative) cost ranges from $435 to $750[34] (depending upon how many products and services one wants to register under the same

---

[34]All data in this chapter respect the United States, which serves as an illustration. Naturally numbers for other regions will vary.

name) and it can go for ever, as there is no expiration date, provided every 10 years the trademark is renamed and proof made that it is still in use.

A second relevant issue **is how to select a name**. And here let's give the word again to Nike's founder Phil Knight:

He needed a name and so a *poll* was taken among all employees: secretaries, accountants, sales reps, retail clerks, warehouse workers, with <u>all</u> required to jump in and make at least <u>one</u> suggestion.

Over the next few days dozens of ideas were kicked around until four leading candidates emerged:

- Falcon;
- Condor;
- Dimension Six; and
- Nike.

Phil Knight lobbied again and again for Dimension Six only to be told by his employees that it was unspeakably bad. It led him to finally agree on Nike.

Athena Nike is the *Greek goddess* of victory: the Acropolis; the Parthenon; Athens. It is **short** (two syllables). And sounds **strong** as all names with the letter K or X do. They stick to mind.

And so *Nike* was born.

This story illustrates *two* things. *First*, great names must preferably be short[35] (two syllables or less) for strength and easy to be remembered: Bic

---

[35]And so Jennifer Anastassakis changed to Jennifer Aniston, Frederick Austerlitz to Fred Astaire, Charles Buchinsky to Charles Bronson, and James Bumgarner to James Garner.

Tonny Bennet was one of the great crooners of the 20th century selling over 50 million records and according to Frank Sinatra the best singer of the kind. His true name? Anthony Benedetto.

(not Bich, the surname of the innovator), Clorox, Kleenex, Xerox. And if possible *with* a K or X for strength: Kit Kat.

Better still if the name **indicates** what the product *does* or stands for: Lite, People (the gossip magazine), Vision Center, Super Glue, Fortune.

Or alternatively what the product is *associated with*: Dove (love, beaty soap), Fuji (the image of Fujiyama, the sacred Japanese mountain under strong blue skies), Duracell (durability in batteries), Federal Express (speed).

And in the case of *Nike, victory*. What's more important, thought Phil Knight, than victory as he recalled **Churchill's** words: *you ask, what is our aim? I can answer in one word: it is victory.*

After all wasn't the victory medal awarded to all veterans of WWII a bronze medallion with Athena Nike on the front?

The Nike story also illustrates that **no single person** should decide upon a name. It is too important for that. Although the final call was on Phil Knight, better to do as he did:

1—Ask for *suggestions*;
2—*Keep only those* that satisfy most if not all of the above criteria (short, strong, associated with the product);
3—Make at least *one more round* among all.[36]

---

[36]The Delphi method can here be useful: after each round, the participants are presented with an aggregated summary of the last round, allowing each person to adjust their answer. Several rounds are done until only one, or very few suggestions are left.

Better to decrease subjectivity, through intersubjectivity, that is the opinion of many, thus leaning toward objectivity. Since "I am not going to be the only customer of my company, it exists not to serve me, but many."

Then besides names, **logos** can and should be *registered for protection*. Preferably *simple* to be memorized; visually *attractive* (to be appealing); and *reinforcing* what the company stands for (together with the name and the rest of the marketing mix).

Chicago, National Sporting Goods Association show: What's this?, asks a sales rep. That's a **swoosh**. The hell's a swoosh? It's the sound of someone going past you. And the sales people loved it. The swoosh is a fluid mark shape that indicates movement and speed.

Developed by Davidson, an outside consultant, for the price of $35, today it is worth $26 billion and is one of the world's most valuable logos.

Marlboro's cowboy stands for manhood, *Volvo*'s child for family security, *Federal Express* plane for air speed, *Patek Philippe*'s son for a watch that is an investment for the next generation, and Nestlé's nest for newborn care.

And the word *Nestlé* is an example that the logo (nest) and name should go together, mutually reinforcing each other. In Swabian (a German dialect of the Alps) Nestlé means (a small bird's) nest.

Just as with names, **logos trademarks** have no expiration date, but must be renewed and proven that they are in use every 10 years. The difference is the lower cost: from $225 to $660 (for name it is between $435 and $750).[37]

---

[37]Again here and henceforth, all data for the United States, which serve as illustration.

And **slogans** (Just do it—Nike; The driving machine—BMW; The legend in adventure—Camel) can also be trademarked as long as they are:

(1) Distinctive;
(2) Used in the market;
(3) Nonfunctional, meaning it should not address an essential characteristic of the product or service (which other brands _also_ address);
(4) Not misleading; and
(5) No conflict (with other trademarks).

In the United States the initial registration term is 10 years, to be renewed indefinitely as long as it is in use.

But at the very early stages of launching a product or service into the market, the slogan is not a priority, if it ever becomes one.

5.2.2. Patents[38]

Six questions are worth analyzing.

When should filing for a patent be done? _Who_ should do it? _How_? _Where_? How much does it _cost_? And how _long_ does it take?

5.2.2.1. When?

The answer is **as soon as** possible. But the focus here is on filing for, and keeping the process **alive**, not necessarily obtaining it, something whose date depends not only on us but also on the patent department.

A final decision can take slightly more than three years: one year for a _provisional_ patent (optional) and over two years for the _definitive_ (also called _utility_) one.

---

[38]Again as the process varies from country to country, here the data of the United States will be analyzed, as an example.

The most essential requirement here is to keep the process **alive and to start it as soon as possible**.

Many very useful innova-tions go unnoticed, as the paper *supermarket bag*. Un-til Margaret Knight came along, its bottom was not square, but angled, and thus able to contain only far fewer items.

Margaret Knight

When **M. Knight** had the idea she placed a first order to a factory, only for the owner himself to find that it was such a great idea that he should patent it, himself. In the lawsuit that followed M. Knight won only be-cause of all the documents she had kept.

Bell is widely known as the inventor of the telephone. However, that is not so. The true inventor a few years before was the Italian Meucci, only that he failed to patent it. So Bell filled the patent in Febru-ary 14, 1876.

And a few hours (too) late another American called Gray arrived at the patent's office with the same purpose…

The lesson here is **twofold**. *First*, the case of M. Knight illustrates the importance of *keeping all documentation* when dealing with third parties and making them sign *nondisclosure agreements*. Just as when building prototypes. And *second*, the importance of applying for a patent *as soon as* one has a prototype or detailed drawings.

Sure enough large companies may be able to patent "around" the inno-vation, but they will be unable to go to the core of the solution, which remains protected.

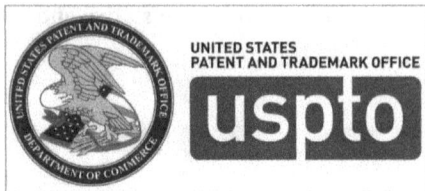

That is why in all TV programs where entrepreneurs present their ideas to venture capitalists or business angels, one of the most common questions is: do you have a patent? And an answer of **pending is enough**. So gung ho. Ask at least for a *provisional patent*.

5.2.2.2. Who Should Do It?

The entrepreneur. If she/he has the time for it. Thus saving (needed) money.

Sara Blakely, founder of the unicorn *Spanx*, working from her apartment, bought a Barnes & Noble textbook and writing the patent application saved $3,000.[39]

There is no need for a patent attorney to submit a provisional patent application (fee between $60 and $200 for micro-entities), which allows for a one-year window to write a definitive (called utility) patent application.

Provisional applications lack many of the formalities of definitive (utility) patent applications, allowing the entrepreneur, patent in hand, to obtain financing and fine-tuning the invention.[40]

---

[39]The website of the U.S. Patent and Trademark Office is also a source of highly valuable information.

[40]A **provisional patent** does not undergo a formal examination by the patent's office and it provides certain benefits during the one-year period following the filing date. These **benefits** include:

1. *Patent pending status*: one can use the phrase "patent pending" or "patent applied for," indicating that the invention is in the process of being patented. That deters potential infringers and provides legal protection;

(continues in the next page)

Filing for a *utility (definitive)* patent is another matter. As the example of Spanx demonstrates that can be done by the entrepreneur, but is more time consuming and difficult.

A **patent lawyer** (who passed an exam, is registered with the patent office, and is frequently specialized in specific industries such as pharmaceuticals, telecommunications, and so on) has the **advantages** of speeding up the process (by anticipating the patent office's obstacles) and bringing expertise into the process (through minimizing omissions and oversights that will limit the scope of the obtained patent).

For example, when patenting a machine it is important not to limit it to the components in use, but include other types that work as well. That will avoid being *patented around*.

However, since patent attorneys are among the highest paid, there is always the common option of asking a lawyer to review or complete the patent application. At the *end*. And *only* that.

SMITH & HOPEN
U.S. REGISTERED PATENT ATTORNEYS

In conclusion, if time is not, but funds are, a restraint, it makes sense to apply for a provisional patent and during one year fine-tune the invention and obtain financing.

---

2. *Priority date*: the filing date of the patent application becomes the priority date. Meaning that if someone else files a similar invention after the first date, one has priority over obtaining a patent.

3. *Additional time* (for development and assessment): the one-year period of provisional patent pending status allows time to further develop the invention, conduct market research, obtain financing, or assess the commercial viability before committing to the cost and effort of filing a non-provisional patent application.

The provisional patent pending status, although providing some benefits, does not grant a patent. For such a purpose, a non-provisional patent application must be done within the one-year period, which will undergo an examination process by a patent examiner.

Advisability of the entrepreneur doing
everything until the final decision

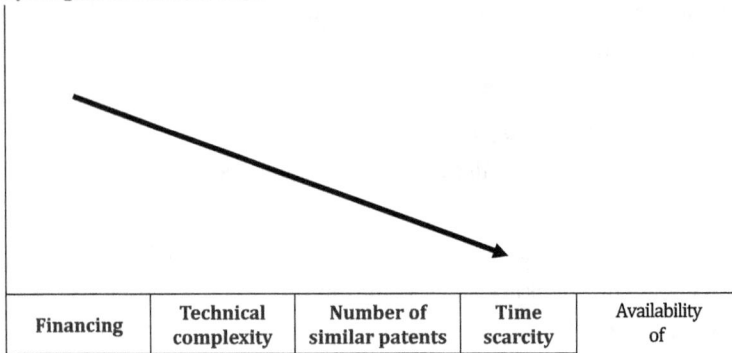

Financing	Technical complexity	Number of similar patents	Time scarcity	Availability of

Figure 17

Then, again depending on **the balance** among (A) *time*, (B) *money*, (C) the *technical complexity*[41] of the invention, and (D) the number of existing *similar* patents the entrepreneur can (as summarized in Figure 17):

1. *Apply* for an utility patent and go all the way until the final decision;

   or

2. *Hire* an attorney to act as a *consultant* reviewing the application and coaching the applicant; or still

3. *Start* the process and *hire* an attorney to complete it; or finally

4. *Hire* an attorney to do the *whole process* from beginning to end.

Finally, if a patent attorney is not required, neither is a prototype, all that is necessary to start the process, to obtain the pending status (provisional or in the utility application), and a final decision are drawings and detailed specifications of the invention, as long as it is new, nonobvious, practical/useful, and never has been in use.

A *prototype* however *facilitates* (an image is worth…). And it is frequently a must for investors and with focus groups. Thus it is highly advisable that a prototype be made.

---

[41] As referred, many patent attorneys are industries specialized.

Then, if an attorney is not a must, but a prototype yes, what else is needed? And **how to** go about it?

5.2.2.3. How?

There are several good sites that help to go through patenting, including that of the U.S. Patent and Trademark Office (USPTO).[42]

At the core of the process is:

a. There are things that **can** (processes, machines, articles) and **cannot** be patented (laws of nature, physical phenomena)—**Figure 18**;

b. Besides products, **services** can also be patented, as long as they are practically useful. Examples are methods for conducting online auctions, online streaming platforms (e.g., Netflix's technology), CRM (customer relationship management), and ride-sharing service (the technology used by Uber);[43]

c. And as said, the **two** main types of patents are provisional (one year) and utility (definitive);

d. To obtain a patent an innovation **must be**:
   • New;
   • Nonobvious;
   • Useful; and
   • Not have been in use;

e. The **steps** in applying are:
   • Conducting a *search* in the USPTO database using increasingly detailed keywords, to make sure the innovation has not yet been patented;
   • *Describing* the invention using a prototype (preferably), drawings, and photographs;

---

[42]Other good sites include: Small Business Innovation Research (www.sbir.gov/tutorials/patents/); LegalZoom (www.legalzoom.com); Google Patents (www.patents.google.com).

[43]Patent protection is also available for ornamental designs of manufacture articles (design patents) and plant patents (newly invented plant).

WHAT CAN AND CANNOT BE PATENTED

What can be patented—utility patents are provided for a new, nonobvious, and useful:
- Processes (of manufacturing, etc)
- Machinery
- Articles of manufacture (toys, appliances, tools, etc)
- Composition of matter
  - Software
  - Business methods
- Improvement of any of the above

What cannot be patented:
- Laws of nature
- Physical phenomena
- Abstract ideas
- Literary, dramatic, musical, and artistic works (these can be Copyright protected)
- Inventions which are:
  - Not useful; or
  - Offensive to public morality.

Source: Site "United States Patent and Trademark Office"

Figure 18

- *Differentiate* the invention from the prior art found; and again generally;
- To apply for a *provisional* rather than a utility patent outright.[44]

The desired outcome is a *20-year*[45] patent, provided the annual fees are paid. In principle, there are no extensions. However, in some instances, if there are delays of the USPTO responsibility, the 20-year[45] period can be extended.

5.2.2.4. Where to Apply?

A country's patent office power is naturally limited to its **geographical boundaries**, and so a patent in the United States (e.g.) gives exclusive rights only to the U.S. market and one by the European Union Intellectual Property Office (EUIPO) solely to the European Union.

---

[44]The process is paved with many intricacies; for instance, one must distinguish between a multiple patent approach (which requires a new patent request every time there is an important alteration) and the prototype approach (where the above is far less necessary).

[45]15 years for design patents and there are other special cases.

Thus, as soon as one is making money (with a regional/national patent pending) and considering the possibility of going abroad,[46] the Patent Cooperation Treaty (linked to the **World Intellectual Property Organization**) should be used, as it allows to file a single application for protection in multiple countries.

Alternatives are using several regional offices such as the European Patent Office.

In any case, qualified patent **attorneys** are now, for international purposes, **a must**.

5.2.2.5. How Much Does It Cost?

One must here distinguish between:

- Administrative (USPTO) and lawyer's fees;
- Initial and total process fees;
- Provisional and utility patents;
- U.S. and international patent (under the Patent Cooperation Treaty/World Organization) fees; and finally
- The fees vary for micro, small, and large entities.

The USPTO considers **three** categories: micro-entities, small entities (the administrative fees are ± double those of micro), and large entities (whose fees are considerably higher).[47] Regarding **lawyers'** fees there are no standard rules.

Figure 19 provides an approximate range of values for **micro-entities**.

---

[46]The previous chapter provided several examples where imports from other geographical areas are frequently a source for local innovation.

[47]A **micro-entity** has an income less than three times the median household income or is associated with high education entities.

PATENT COST (IN DOLLARS FOR MICRO-ENTITIES)			
Type / Stage	USA		International (Patent Cooperation Treaty)
	Provisional	Utility	
Administrative — Application	60–200	65–700	1,435
Administrative — Prosecution and conclusion		550–1,200	600–3,500
Lawyers (estimate)	2,500–15,000	5,000–20,000	5,000–25,000
Total	2,560–15,200	5,615–21,900	7,035–29,935[1]

(1) – These costs are just to complete the international phase of the process. After the international phase it is necessary to submit an application in each country (under the Patent Cooperation Treaty) where one wants to seek patent protection and it will be required to comply with their individual patent laws, procedures and costs.

Figure 19

The **administrative fees** for a provisional patent are in the range $60 to $200; for an utility one, the application is $65 to $700, and the prosecution and conclusion $550 to $1,200. Lawyers can represent an overcost of $2,500 to $15,000 for provisional and of $5,000 to $20,000 for utility patents.

International patents are far more expensive. The application fee is $1,435, for prosecution and conclusion $600 to $3,500, and attorney fees range between $5,000 and $25,000.

While within the United States, fees change with the type of entity, internationally they are standard.

And at least part of the funding can come from **crowdfunding** and then **business angels**.

The Ice Cream Canteen (pint size container to keep the temperature) used Kickstarter for crowdfunding and obtained 1,882 backers in exchange for the product.

Then the entrepreneur in the TV program Shark Tank got $100,000 and $200,000 loan in exchange for 20 percent equity.

5.2.2.6. How Long Does It Take?

Provisional patents last for one year and the average time for a *utility* patent is around two years and two months.

5.2.2.7. Concluding Remarks on Patents

Patenting (<u>filing for</u>) is a **must**, although (1) *expensive*, (2) *hard work*, and (3) *cumbersome*. These are three drawbacks.

Consolation should come however equally from **three** sources. *First* the **protection** patents provide. *Second*, the far lower price of **provisional** patents (between $60 and $200), which offers a one-year "moratorium" to obtain financing either from sales or investors. And *finally*, Americans can take further solace from the fact that the U.S. system is one of the **fastest and cheapest in the world**.[48]

As referred at this chapter's beginning it was not Bell who invented the telephone. It was Meucci, in Italy a few years earlier. He invented but did not patent it. Why? He simply could not afford it.

Alexander Bell   Antonio Meucci

5.3. Setting the Price of the Innovation

Helmut Maucher, the well-known former president of *Nestlé*, said in his 2007 book *Management Brevier*[49] *that one does not know much about pricing.*

---

[48]Another advantage of the U.S. system is that all inventions must be made public, thus facilitating licensing.
[49]Campus Verlag; 2007.

Since then prospect theory/behavioral economics brought major advancements[50] and the best and most straightforward method for an entrepreneur **to start** pricing is the **bottom-up method**.

The method involves **10** steps as in the example below, which uses simple numbers to illustrate.

First, what is the future entrepreneur's *present salary* or best expected future offer?[51] That's the starting point. Let's assume, for the sake of simplicity, 5,000 per month, making an annual value of 60 (5 × 12 months).[52]

Second, new ventures are both risky and very hardworking. Thus, they deserve at least a 100 percent *risk premium* and compensation for extra work. At the very least. Thus, 60 × 2 = 120.

Third, there are *taxes*. If (e.g.) corporate[53] taxes are 30 percent, that implies profit before taxes must be 170 (120 divided by 0.7).

Fourth, what are the *fixed costs* (rent, part-time help, and so on)? Three thousand per month? That makes 36 a year. Adding up to 170 totals 206.

Fifth, what is the *most similar* good to the innovation?

---

[50]A booming field with many worthwhile titles. One of the most transversal and practical is the book: *Misbehaving* (Penguin Random House, 2015) by Nobel Prize winner Richard Thaler. And Dan Ariely has many outstanding books as well, including *Predictably Irrational.*

[51]Henceforth all values are in thousands.

[52]In some countries employees are paid 13, 14, and more months per year. They also expect bonus and other variable compensation. If so, the total value should be adjusted to take all types of remunerations into consideration.

[53]Depending upon the law and tax system of each country, entrepreneurs may pay corporate, income, or no taxes (during the start-up phase) at all.

If the innovation is Pencil Bugs, the answer is standard pencils. In the case of Enamorata (the beach towel which has embedded an insect repellent), it is standard beach towels.

In the case of Hamboards (surfing boards with wheels to simulate inland sea surfing), it is the skates.

Transparent toasters? "Normal," opaque toasters. Price Jones (sleeping bags that come with a cushion and double as blankets)? "Standard" sleeping bags. Baby Toon? A simple silicone toy. Ice Cream Canteen? Portable freezers. Spanx? Full-sized control-top pantyhoses.

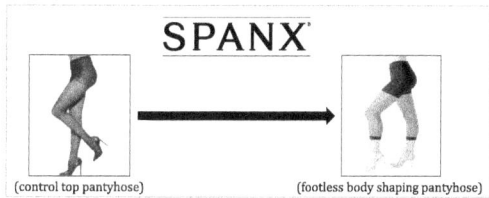

(control top pantyhose)   (footless body shaping pantyhose)

Sixth, what are the *annual sales of the most similar product* within the geographic boundaries of the innovation, or patent coverage?

Let's assume 330,000.

Seventh, what is the *direct cost* of each unit of the innovation produced?

By direct cost is meant the purchasing price to the best supplier.

The selection criteria can be proximity, reliability, acceptance of small orders, speed, or cost. Whatever. Nike suppliers' location evolved successively, from Japan and New Jersey, to New Mexico, Taiwan, South Korea, and finally China.

The assumption is that *all production will be outsourced.* If however a part of it is done indoors, whatever the internal costs are, they should be added to the cost of goods sold.

How much a supplier will charge depends of course on the size of the order, which leads to the next step.

Eight, as there are *economies of scale* (the cost decreases with quantity due to, among other reasons, fixed costs) it is important to know how the cost varies according to the size of the order.

In the first year an entrepreneur (to be in safe ground) should not assume to sell more than **3 percent** of the most similar product (Pencil Bugs—all pencils; Enamorata—all beach towels; and so forth).

There is always resistance to innovation, the fear of the unknown. And so better to err for underthan overestimation of sales (one can go only up). And the smaller the annual sales, the higher the direct cost, forcing again any surprises, now on cost, to be on the positive side.

Thus since the expectation is in the first year to sell 10,000 (3 percent of the market annual sales of 330,000), how much does our chosen supplier charge?

If the direct cost is five, the cost of goods sold (direct costs) is 50(000).

Then (ninth), *adding* 50 to the value of 206 of the fourth step above amounts to a total cost of 256(000).

Tenth: since the expected (annual) sales are 10, the price must be **26**, so that $26 \times 10 = 260$, the minimum value to cover 256 of total costs.

In short, a price of **26**, for (annual) sales of *10*, gives a sales value of *260*, and taking direct costs of *50* into consideration, the difference is *206*, which after fixed costs of *36* and taxes of *50* creates a bottom line of *120*, twice the value of the present or expected future salary of the entrepreneur to be.

The **bottom-up method**, although direct and simple, has **two caveats**:

To start with, the *timeframe* for setting the price is *one-year sales*, but in practice, orders will come in **smaller quantities** during the year, implying higher prices from the suppliers.

Again the solution is straightforward. To obtain quotations for different quantities from the chosen supplier(s) and for each order to adjust the selling price of 26 accordingly (always up).

That means that the price of 26 (for a forecasted year sales of 10,000) acts as a minimum, a floor, bringing also the advantage that customers will have different selling prices for distinct order quantities, just as they would expect.

Also, there is nowadays in the United States and other developed countries some antagonism against outsourcing geographically, as it implies **exporting jobs**.

The way out is also simple. To get a cost quotation **both** from an overseas and an American, a local, supplier. And then to price the product accordingly: one price if the product is made outside; another if internally, with total guarantee to the customer that whatever the case the product is absolutely equal. And so if the customer raises the issue of where the good is manufactured, simply offer the two options and ask to choose.

5.4. Last Tests Before Going Ahead

So far after having identified unsolved **problems** that constitute **opportunities** (Chapter 2), they were in the **inquire** part of PISA (Chapter 3), submitted to **six** tests:

1. *Frequency*;
2. *Relevance*;

3. *Focus*;
4. *No other solution* exists to get the job done;
5. Behavioral interviews tested people's *actions*; and
6. Direct emotional assessment to evaluate *feelings*.

Then (7) a solution was created. A (8) prototype made. A (9) patent applied for. And (10) a price set. And thus the innovation is now finally ready **to be launched into the market**.

However, if one wishes, **four** further **additional tests** may eventually be useful before the go-ahead:

- *Price-to-cost ratio;*
- *Break-even analysis;*
- *Level of competitive advantage;* and
- *Query on the anonymous client.*

These tests provide additional useful information on the *likelihood of success*.

5.4.1. The Price-to-Cost Ratio

While setting the price in the previous section, it stood out that there are basically **two** distinct types of costs: **internal and external**.

The *latter* are the price at which one buys from suppliers; the *former* includes besides the entrepreneur salary other costs such as rent, utilities, and salaries of helping hands.

Trivial Pursuit

And their **flexibility** is different. While cost is a major factor in carefully selecting the supplier, cost flexibility is greater in internal than external costs.

Indeed, for a short period the entrepreneur can—if need be—decrease his/her salary; also ask for temporary sacrifices from the start-up team (frequently enthusiasts of the new venture as in Trivial Pursuit); move into more modest installations; and so on.

That means if the beginning is harder than thought beforehand, the **cushion** will come far easier from internal than external costs.

Thus, when the ratio of selling price to cost of purchase is **high**, a **safe net** exists. When **low**, it does **not**.[54]

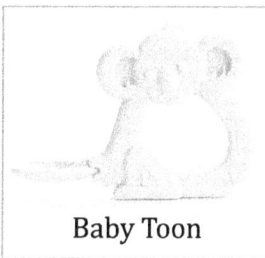

Baby Toon

In the previous section example, the price was 26 and the direct cost 5, making for a ratio of 5.2. Baby Toon costs 6.6 to produce and is sold to retailers at 15 for a ratio of 2.2.

The seat gap filler (Drop Stop) has a ratio of 2.5; the SockTabs is four[55]; Ice Cream Canteen cost is 7.5 and its selling price online is 35 (a discount from the standard 45 price), thus a ratio of 4.7.[56]

Ice Cream Canteen

The ratio varies with the industry and within it with the segment. The **global average** in the restaurant industry is around **three**. But cheaper outlets use two and fancier ones four and luxury ones far more. The ratio here is called price to food costs.

---

[54]The reverse of dividing the price over cost (cost divided by price) is usually called the percentage of cost of goods sold.

[55]Seat gap filler (Drop Stop): production cost of 4; retailer cost of 10; consumer cost of 20, making 1 – 2.5 – 5.

SockTabs: production cost 1.25; retailer cost 5; consumer price of 10; thus 1 – 4 – 8.

[56]If the good is sold directly to the final consumer through TV, the internet, or any other form of direct sales, what counts is the price to the final customer. But when sold to retail, the important is the selling price to it. In other words, **who pays**? The retailer? That's what matters. The final consumer? That's what counts. Moreover the price should be net, after all types of discounts and commissions.

In general, **cross section to the whole economy**, the global **average** is in between **2.5** and **3.3** (percentage of cost of goods sold of 30–39 percent): 1 (cost), 3 (price—direct or to the distributor[57]), and 6 (the consumer selling price of the retailer): 1 – 3 – 6.

Thus, the **higher the price-to-cost** ratio (the lower the percentage of cost of goods sold) the **better**. And if the ratio is above 2.5 it is generally **within the interval** of the whole economy and thus a good sign. It is not below average.

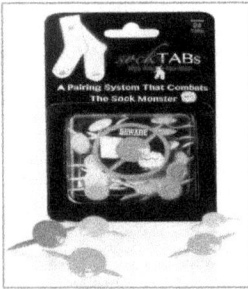

So, Baby Toon with a 2.2 ratio falls below the 2.5 minimum. Seat gap filler (Drop Stop) is just on the edge, at the lower end of the economy average range (2.5). And above that are the SockTabs (4), Ice Cream Canteen (4.7), and the example of the last section (5.2).

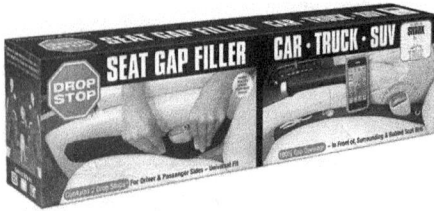

Anyway the ratio value of **2.5** although nonbinding provides **useful** information to be completed with that of other tests (that follow).

5.4.2. Break-Even Analysis

In the example of the previous section forecasted sales were 10,000 units, corresponding to the 3 percent benchmark of the total market, creating a profit of 120,000, double the present or near future entrepreneur's wage.

But what are the **minimum** sales volume not to lose money? To **"zero" profit**?

The answer is given by diving the level of fixed costs (36,000) by the unit margin of 21 (price of 26 minus direct cost of 5), giving a result of 1,714 units.

---

[57] The longest chain is wholesaler—transporter—retailer—consumer.

That is **1/6** of the expected (benchmark) sales of 10,000.[58]

A very low ratio. Thus a small risk. And creating a cushion, a safety net.

On the contrary, the closer the break-even value is to the expected benchmarked sales, the worse.[59]

5.4.3. Competitive Advantage

It may also be useful to compare the innovation to the **best close substitute** on how well both get the job done. How do they compare in **competence**?

Let's look at **two** examples, with increasing degree of complexity.

It will be recalled that **Enamorata** is the beach towel that comes with an insect repellent chemical embedded in it.

What's the best alternative? **A spray**. And what do customers **want** in both instances?

First of all they want that insects are indeed **repelled**. Thus in a scale of one (minimum importance) to five (maximum importance) that receives an evaluation of five.

Next, to avoid **bothering** others is rated as a four in relevance. And **smell** and **practicality** receive a three and a two, close to minimum relevance.

The key factors (qualities the product must have) are defined by clients in a *net survey*, to be described next. If others (e.g., fear of cancer) were indicated they should naturally be included.

---

[58]And 0.5 percent of the 330,000 total market: five in 1,000.

[59]To be noted that profit here includes (the double of) the entrepreneur wage. If one wants to consider profit beyond the (two) wages, then the break-even is … 3 percent of the market equal to 10,000 units of sales. If beyond one wage, 1.5 percent of the market (5,000 units); and so on.

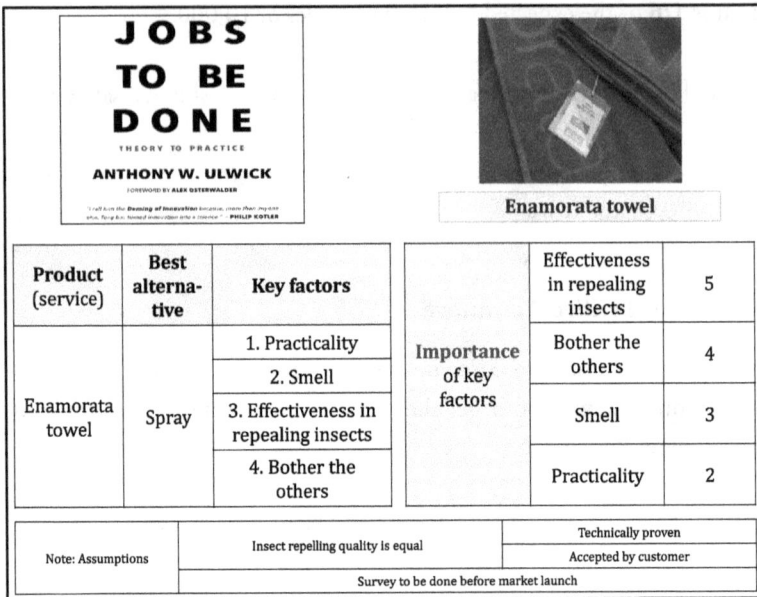

Product (service)	Best alternative	Key factors			
				Effectiveness in repealing insects	5
Enamorata towel	Spray	1. Practicality	Importance of key factors	Bother the others	4
		2. Smell			
		3. Effectiveness in repealing insects		Smell	3
		4. Bother the others		Practicality	2

Note: Assumptions	Insect repelling quality is equal	Technically proven
		Accepted by customer
	Survey to be done before market launch	

Figure 20 Key required factors for competence

In any case, besides the key requirements, there is another distinct issue: **how well** do both the spray and the Enamorata perform in the requirements? How competent are they?

The answer is given in **Figure 21.**

Both spray and Enamorata are evaluated as doing an *equally* good job in repelling insects and so they both receive a **four** in the five-point scale. But they are quite *different* in the extent of bothering others: the spray is terrible (and thus receives a one) and the towel great (and therefore a five).

Then there is practicality and smell. Here again Enamorata is judged as *highly competent* (a five in both instances) while the spray is evaluated *poorly* (one for practicality and three for smell).

We thus have the information on how important each requirement is to get the job done (on a scale of one to five) and how well each product complies with and accomplishes each requirement.

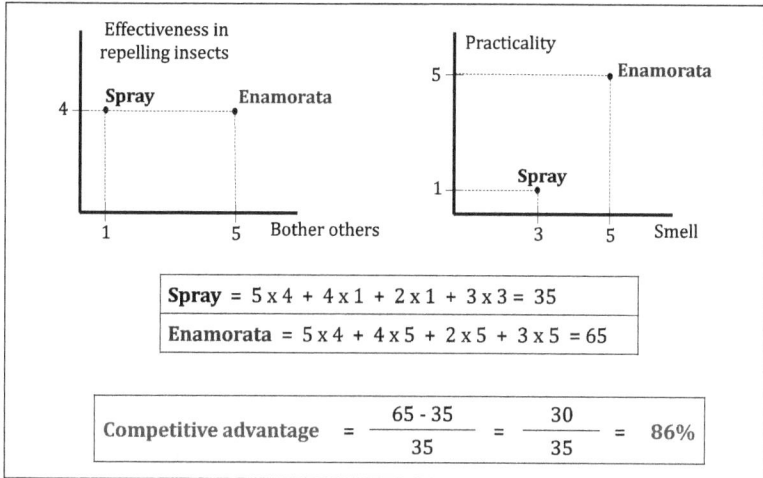

Figure 21 Competence level of spray and Enamorata

Thus multiplying the importance by the competence as in **Figure 21**, one obtains an overall **competence level** for each of the two products.

The spray competence level is **35** and that of Enamorata is **65**.

Thus Enamorata is nearly **twice better** than the spray: 65 less 35 divided by 35 gives 86 percent. It has almost the double "productivity". It creates two times the level of satisfaction near the clients. That is called its **competitive advantage**.

In this example, there is one best substitute (the spray) to the innovation (Enamorata). But **what if there is not only a best substitute but a few?**[60]

Then, one compares the innovation with the **average** rating of the best substitutes as per

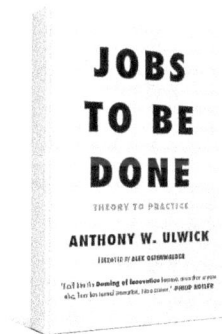

_____

[60]The decision of comparing with one, two, or more alternatives is facilitated by looking at, on top of the concept, the market share.

NORTH AMERICAN CIRCULAR SAW MARKET

1	2	3	4	$\boxed{4} - \boxed{3}\, \text{x}\, \boxed{2}$
Desired outcomes (on a scale of zero to ten)	Importance	Average satisfaction with established brands	Satisfaction with innovation	
Minimize debris flying up	9	3	6	+54
Minimize likelihood of moving off the cut line	8	6	5	-8
Minimize likelihood of snagging the cord	7	6	8	+14
Minimize time to put saw back in service when power cord is cut	6	6	6	0

Competitive advantage of innovation:

$$\frac{\text{Difference of total competence levels between innovation and average of competition:}}{\text{Total competence level of competition:}} = +40\%$$

Difference of total competence levels between innovation and average of competition:
$$+54 - 8 + 14 = +60$$
Total competence level of competition:
$$9\text{x}3 + 8\text{x}6 + 7\text{x}6 + 6\text{x}6 = 153$$

= +40%

Figure 22

Figure 22, which compares a new circular saw against the average of the three best established brands in the market.[61]

The **first column** presents the requirements that the customers expect to be satisfied. The **second** the importance the clients attribute to each requirement (now on a scale of one—low importance, to ten—great importance). The **third column** indicates how competent in average the (e.g., three) established brands are in performing each requirement and the **fourth column** the competence level of the innovation, of the new circular saw.

Again by multiplying the importance (of the requirements) by the satisfaction provided by the alternatives, a value for total competence level is obtained.

And when comparing both competence levels, the conclusion is that the innovation of the new circular saw is 40 percent better than the brands

---

[61] This example is a simplification of *Jobs To Be Done* by A. W. Ulwick; Idea Bite Press, 2016.

already in the market: +40 percent (in the case of Enamorata it was 86 percent, nearly the double). That, again, is the **competitive advantage**.

The **final question** is: who provides the information on both the requirements to get the job done and how competent is each product? And the answer is the present customers and/or the target clients of the innovation.

The remaining aspects of how best to organize the data collection, sample size, and cost were already analyzed in Section 3.5 of Chapter 3 when discussing behavioral interviews.

There it was recommended online survey sites such as Momentive/SurveyMonkey or SurveySparrow, for sample size the use of calculators online, and the cost charged varies, but for example it is about \$380 for 10 answers from 100 participants.[62]

The bottom line is **twofold**. The higher the **competitive advantage**, the better. And if the innovation is rated as having a competitive disadvantage by underperforming the alternatives, and so the comparison produces a negative value (instead of a positive one, namely +86 percent and +40 percent), then the advisability of launching it into the market is **highly questionable**. At the very least.

5.4.4. Anonymous Client

A final test, using the above-mentioned sites may still be done.

To a sample of clients (of the closest substitute or target customers) **one asks:** *how likely it is that they will buy the innovation? Definitely? Probably? Perhaps? Unlikely? Or definitely not?*

---

[62]Provided one indicates the confidence level (probability of being true), the range (size of the interval the true value must fall into), and the population size. In practice, always more than 30, best 100, and never necessary more than 10 percent of the target market.

With **anonymous** answers what is the **percentage** that answer **definitely**? A common benchmark is to expect that at least **half** will say they will (1) acquire (2) definitely the new product or service.

The benchmark of half is needed, because in spite of the anonymity and thus expecting independence and sincerity, more likely than not, respondents tend to be sympathetic to the new product and to the surveyor paying them, and thus are overoptimistic about their use.

Naturally, instead of using the internet, an **in-person** focus group is an alternative to obtain a firsthand reaction to the product. But it has *two disadvantages*. The even greater likelihood of unwanted friendliness and optimism if composed of friends and the cost if constituted by strangers.

5.4.5. Overview of the above Four Final Tests

On top of the tests of the **inquire** phase of PISA, it may be **useful** to perform **four** others:

- The **price-to-cost ratio** (the higher the better and with a level of at least **2.5**, which is the bottom level of the average interval in the economy);
- The **break-even analysis** (the lower the ratio compared to **3 percent** of market sales, the better);
- **Competitive advantage** (preferably **high** and never **negative**); and
- The **anonymous clients**: will at least **50 percent** say they will **definitely** acquire the innovation?

That should be done with the help of a **focus group** (online or in-person) as analyzed in the next and last two sections of this chapter.

5.5. Focus Group

If you wish to go fast, go alone; if you wish to go a long distance, go with others, so says the African proverb.

Thus the importance of a focus group to accompany market entry, the objective here being twofold. First, with a prototype in hand to advise on **improvements**. And second to suggest **new models**.

Improvements[63] respect **three** issues:

- Does it really **work**?
- Which qualities to **add**?
- How to solve the **inconveniences**?

Pencil Bugs: how excited are the kids in obtaining the whole collection?

And what about little girls with *fish flops*: sandals with a fish design, hats, t-shirts, and children's books? Do they really care about the whole collection or just shrug it off?

And small girls and boys about pole spikes to climb trees?

---

[63]Improvement is a continuous evolving process. Until Harland Sanders of **KFC** settled on the "final" chicken recipe he went on to add 11 different herbs and spices. And of course if the recipe was final that was not the end, as a new beginning started by adding different items (nuggets), flavors (extra crispy), formats (sandwiches), side dishes (mashed potatoes, green beans, sweet kernel corns, drinks), bucket sizes, combinations, and so on.

Then which **qualities to add**? For instance regarding *Hamboards*, the surfing board on wheels that simulates on land the sea experience: wheels (type, size, place, and number)?; and on the board itself (length, type of wood, and improvements on finishing)?

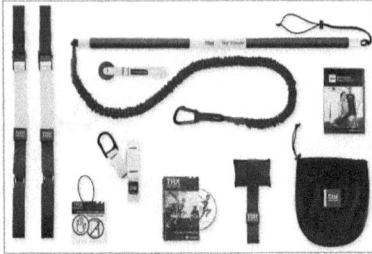

The *TRX* started as two simple rubber strips[64] to be used in exercises pulling from doors, trees, and poles. But then, one by one, extras were added.

Next comes the **defects:** the Ice Cream Canteen (the pint size ice cream freezer) is a success with year sales near half a million and net profit representing 50 percent of sales.

But from the start it was far from perfect with several **inconveniences**, including frequently the pots coming with dents, not tall enough to be able to keep the ice cream lid, and its performance (the four hours capacity of keeping the ice cream frozen) being worse with softer ice cream.

And regarding product shortcomings, it makes no difference if they are real or perceived. Perception is reality in terms of consumers' behavior as they act not according to facts but to opinions. Thus the importance of:

- On *Enamorata*, is there a certification by an independent credible entity that the chemical in the towel does not cause cancer?
- Who certifies that *Bumpsters* (the cloths protecting infants from injuring themselves in bed) are porous enough to avoid suffocation?
- The *pole climbing spikes* are a 100 percent nonslip tool to climb trees? One hundred percent safe?

---

[64]The first prototype was made of parachute leftovers in a military warehouse.

- And *Safetytat*, the children tattoos, are absolutely not toxic? Zero skin allergies?

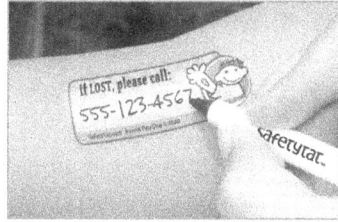

These are the concerns to be addressed in the communications to the market and the instructions accompanying the product.

Thus **Michele Welsh**, the Safetytat inventor, makes clear that:

- It does not erase by water, friction, and so on;
- It does indeed disappear with washing after two days; and
- It has no harmful effects, whatsoever.

Michele Welsh

So **focus groups** must address these **three** types of improvements: does the innovation really **work**? Which qualities to **add**? And what are (the real or perceived) **defects**?

But then they have **another** major utility: to suggest **developing new models**, each for a slightly different need.

Chawel started as a five in one: a beach towel, a garment to change clothes, a sleeping bag, a blanket, and an airplane pillow.

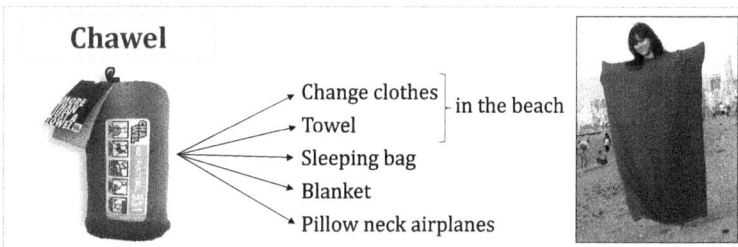

Chawel

Change clothes ⎤
Towel   ⎦ in the beach
Sleeping bag
Blanket
Pillow neck airplanes

But with time it evolved into *two* sizes of *three* different models: sportive for beaches, lakes, and rivers; traveler for camping and mountaineering; and the hybrid, an in-between model.

Models (3) / Sizes (2)	Sportive (beach + lake + river)	Traveler (camping + mountaineering)	Hybrid – in-between
Average			
Big			

Here focus groups can be of considerable help, provided that they address details, not generalities. And the fact that they are time consuming is the price to pay for them to be worthwhile.

How can a company making cleaning sponges be worth $700 million? And sell the sponge for $4 when the lowest priced sponge costs only $1? Don't sponges just absorb and clean? And so are they all basically the same?

Sure, but *Scrub Daddy* added its special chemistry[65] that makes it adequate to clean both soft (e.g., glasses) and hard (e.g., BBQ grills) surfaces, including several other features:

- A **round**-shaped cute face easy to handle;
- Two **holes** (imitating eyes) to wipe out fingers;
- A "**mouth**" to clean both sides of spoons; and
- An attractive, livable **color** of yellow.

---

[65]Which was not invented by the entrepreneur Aaron Krause, but was already in use for industrial, at factory level, purposes. Another example that solutions can be imported from other needs.

In sum, details are the realm of focus groups, illustrating again that small things make great differences and that both God and the devil are in the details. **Winston Churchill** used to say that *what you attribute to my luck does not exist; it is my attention to details.*

But with details in mind **how best to create** focus groups?

The easiest way is to identify friends in need of the innovation, offer each one a prototype, and periodically call them to discuss their use.

To bring them together (in person or online) is **another** possibility. Although far more difficult, it has the great advantage of synergy and serendipity, as one comment leads to another and new ideas emerge.

A **third** possibility is a carefully chosen group of strangers, all potential consumers of the product. Although more reliable for their neutrality, this option is far more expensive. Specially if done in person and not online.

Among all these three alternatives and as frequently, the lower the cost, the less the quality and thus potential for usefulness.

Friends' kindness makes them biased toward optimism and shy on criticism. Interacting with the focus members one by one instead of together prevents consensus building and is less conducive to the generation of new ideas. And although online use is a great saving device of time and money there is no substitute for the in-person contacts.

It is thus frequently most sensible **to evolve** from the first, to the second, to the third alternative modes and so on, as the innovation progresses and finance becomes less of a restraint[66] (**Figure 23**).

---

[66]There are several other ways of obtaining information such as communities, blogs, creating a website, and asking for feedback. However, their informality makes them less productive than more formal focus groups.

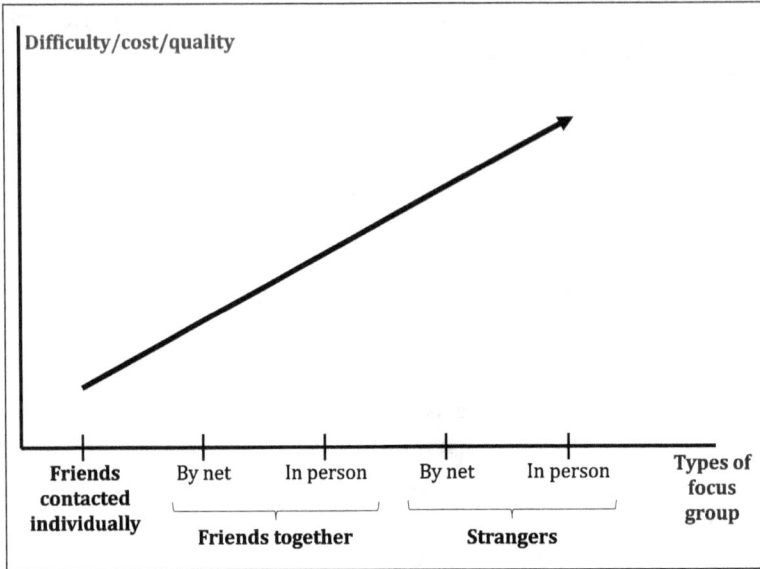

Figure 23 Degree of difficulty/cost/quality of four types of focus groups

But **whatever the type** of focus group **three** aspects are paramount.

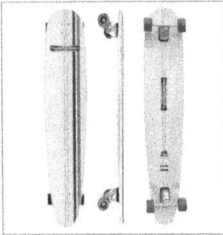

First members must be all **potential (target) consumers**: for Hamboards, surfers. For Pillow Pets (stuffed animals that double as pillows), mothers with young children; for Kangaroos (sneakers with pockets for keys and change), joggers.

Second, regardless of the focus group members being friends or strangers, it is advantageous to make them **financially interested** in the success of the new venture and on top of whatever they are paid for in each session.

The **last** requirement is to **have Cassandras** or **promotor fidei** in the group.

Alfred Sloan, former president of **General Motors** and generally considered one of the best managers of the 20th century, asked once in a board meeting: "so, I take we are all in agreement?" And when everybody nodded, he added, "Then I suggest we adjourn the decision until the next meeting so that we create dissent among us and therefore become aware of the **drawbacks** of the decision."

The only way to make sure our focus group is not biased in favor of the innovation is to include in the group **Cassandras** or **promotor fidei**.

Cassandra is a character from Greek mythology, daughter of King Priam and Queen Hecuba of Troy.

Cassandra became a young woman of magnificent beauty and prophetess, although considered crazy when trying to communicate to the Trojan population countless predictions of catastrophe and doom.

Cassandra was the daughter of Priam, king of Troy, and the origin of the expression prophet of disgrace. All her predictions were of catastrophe and doom.

For centuries the Catholic Church when analyzing the merits of someone to be sanctified would designate a **promotor of fidei** whose only task was to collect all types of evidence that the person under analysis rather than sanctified was indeed ... the devil in person.

That focus group include at least two or three naggers is an absolute must. Pessimists, defeatists, able only to see the dark side of things.

St. Peter's Basilica, Rome

The **promoter** of faith (*promotor fidei*), popularly known as the devil's advocate, is appointed by ecclesiastical authorities to argue against the canonization of a candidate. His job is to have a **sceptical** attitude towards the whole process and focus on **weak points** of the evidence in favour of canonization (especially miracles); and then look for facts and examples that put the candidate's character **in question**.

Their "job" is to point out not only that the whole world is lost but also that there is no way that the innovation product will ever thrive, given its numberless handicaps and therefore produce certain ruin to the entrepreneur. And not only one devil's advocate but **several** so that they cannot be easily silenced.

5.6. Clear Definition of Failure

Strange as it may seem, it is useful to have a clear definition of failure when entering the market, which raises four questions: **what** is meant by that? The **reason** for it? Why **before** market entry? And **how** to do it?

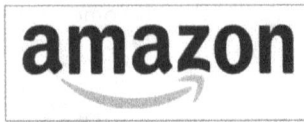

Amazon is known for the number of its innumerous new ventures. But they also always have a clear definition of failure: they pull the plug quickly if the desired outcome is not achieved.

In 2015 it opened an online travel agency (OTA) whose purpose was to book hotels and restaurants within driving distance (not flight options), only for **six** months later to close it for failing to achieve the target share due to the strength of competitors Trip Advisor and Expedia.

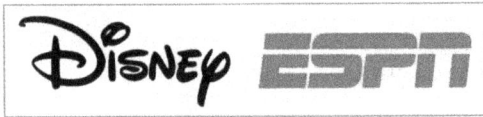

Disney ESPN, the pay TV for 24 hours sports events, in September 2006 launched a mobile version with a specific phone (Sanyo) at the cost of $400 (for the phone) and $40 (the monthly fee). The projected investment was $150 million and the goal to achieve 240,000 subscribers.

However, after **six** months it had only 10,000 subscribers. It took then several corrective actions: decreased the price; increased promotion; and enlarged customer incentives.

Results did not improve significantly. So in September 2007 (**one year** after the launch) it discontinued the service, at the loss of $135 million. Or should one say with saving $15 million from the forecasted investment of $150 million?

Thus a definition of failure is a **quantified event**, a *number*, which if not met by a given *date* will imply pulling the plug on the project.

But isn't that contrary to **perseverance?** The answer is no since **stopping and giving up** are distinct concepts. To persevere is one thing; to repeat mistakes another.

I'm convinced that about half of what separates the successful entrepreneurs from the non-successful ones is pure perseverance, said **Steve Jobs**. And indeed life hit Steve Jobs with a brick many times. He was forced to leave Apple. In 1985 there were serious problems with Next. In 1990 Pixar downsized. And soon later the Wall Street Journal announced that he was doomed. Only for a few years later Jobs return to Apple, save the company, and revolutionize three industries: information systems, telecommunications, and music.

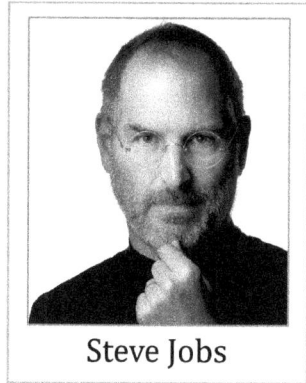

Steve Jobs

Elon Musk built his empire by never stopping. Riley, former wife, counts that in 2008 he looked like death itself and she was thinking he would have a heart attack. Nights meant constant nightmares and Musk would climb on her and start screaming while asleep.

Phil Knight courted bankruptcy year after year. First, a hostile takeover by the Japanese supplier. Then followed a lawsuit. Next, U.S. Customs were bringing Nike under with a fine of $25 million. And years in a row cash strapped (from 1964 to 1980).

Thus *success is going from failure to failure without ever stopping*, noted Winston Churchill. And the motto of Nobel laureate Camilo Cella was *those who persevere, win*.

So **perseverance is fine**. However **Einstein** defined **madness** as *to keep on doing the same things and expect different results* and thus **Phil Knight** calls charlatans the apostles of never giving up: *Those who urge entrepreneurs never to give up? Charlatans. Sometimes you have to give up. Sometimes knowing when to give up, when to try something else is genius. Giving up doesn't mean stopping. Don't ever stop.*

Peter Drucker

In **Drucker's** words: *try, try and try again and do your best; but if after 1/2/3 years it does not work, change gears.*[67] Instead of being drawn into an ever deeper hole because one does not stop digging. When in a hole? Stop digging.

And change[68] can relate to any of the sides of the outer strategic square of **Figure 12** of Chapter 4. Per order of increasing likelihood and thus of sequence: (1) *geography*; (2) *client* type; (3) *need*/model; and finally (4) *product*.

The above examples illustrate that new ventures' **success** requires both **perseverance and giving up**. And that the way to conciliate both is with **change**.

Elmer Doolin and **Herman Lay** were both in the ice cream business. After years of mediocre performance Doolin met a Mexican willing to sell his corn chips business. And at about the same time Lay acquired a potato chips company. They closed their ice cream businesses and made a joint venture to have exclusive rights to sell

---

[67]Which requires **strength**. Never to be confused with **energy** as the former German chancellor *Adenauer* once told *H. Kissinger*. Perseverance is energy. Change is strength. The weak never give up when they should (*Cardinal Ratz*), although to live to fight another day sometimes requires running away (*Musarum Delicate*).
[68]Every single day the world changes. And regardless of change, experience brings new information. **If I were to decide today, would I still repeat what I did in the past?**
No? What then to do about that? (Peter Drucker).
Change is a symptom not of mistake in the past but of capacity of adaptation to the future. Thus the only mistake is not to change, as it is worse to err the times in management than in grammar.

both products in the different U.S. states they operated. Today's result is the second largest business of Pepsico with sales near $20 billion and that is just in the United States and Canada. The name is of course **Frito-Lay**.

In short, to win is to choose the battles.[69]

But why having a clear definition of failure **before** entering the market?

The reason is avoiding the trap of going on and on and on, in the hope that things are just about to turn around. At the next corner.

The booming field of **behavioral economics** calls that **minimization of regrets**.

While proverbs abound (don't cry over spilt milk; let bygones be bygones; one can't change the past; past waters do not move mills; and so on), people just don't follow them as *they do not maximize utility but minimize regrets* and so **sunk costs** should not, but do indeed really, **in practice matter**.

I have a tennis elbow? I will not play if invited, but I will if I already prepaid the lesson.

I have a ticket for a game and a snowstorm comes. If the ticket was offered, I do not go. If I bought it, I go anyway.

I have shoes that hurt my feet. The more expensive they are, the harder it is to give up wearing them.

A CEO has a new car project whose R&D costs 100. When 90 has already been spent, a competitor launches a better model. Most CEOs spend the last 10 anyway.

---

[69]When during the Korean war the U.S. general *O. Smith* was questioned by a journalist why he was retreating, he answered: "I'm not retreating, I'm just moving to attack in another direction."

But if asked: (1) zero has been spent so far; (2) a competitor launches a better model; and (3) R&D costs 10; then (4) most CEOs would not go ahead spending the 10.

Thus, although **sunk costs** should not count in decisions, as bygones are bygones and makes no sense to throw good money on top of bad one, people, by trying to minimize regrets, make sunk costs matter and that pushes entrepreneurs on and on and on in the perpetual hope that the turnaround is just around the corner. And so *to avoid that, a clear definition of failure is necessary at the moment of market entry.*

But **what** should that definition be?

A **distinction** should be first made between the cases of new ventures of established companies (**intrapreneurship**)[70] and the start-ups of individuals (**entrepreneurship**).

---

[70] The above examples of Amazon and Disney respect intrapreneurship. There, the objective goes beyond not losing money. It is also not to pursue businesses that being less profitable than the rest of the portfolio create an **opportunity cost** and decrease the overall profitability of the company. Better to concentrate the scarce resources on the most profitable businesses.

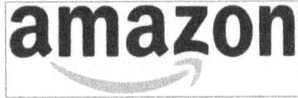

That is what **Peter Drucker** called **planned abandonment: if I were to decide now would I go into the businesses I am in?** And if the answer is no, then divest in order to concentrate all resources in the most promising venues. The first step to grow is to decide what to abandon.

In planned abandonment there are two frequent definitions of failure.

The first is rentability (profits defined by assets), to divest whenever the new venture is consistently far below that of the rest of the portfolio: 10 percent? 15 percent?

The second, used by **Jack Welch** while at the helm of General Electric, is to divest all new businesses that were not number one or two in terms of market share (to avoid new venture managers

from defining the market too narrowly it was required that they define it in such a way that market share was always equal or below 10 percent).

(continues in the next page)

And then still in the latter case one should differentiate between innovations that are **technically complex** and/or requiring **heavy investments** (as those of E. Musk, SpaceX, Tesla, Solar City, or Boring) where longer break-even and payback periods may be accepted and those of **PISA** that are technically **simple** (although of high value): Gymshark, Gousto, Spanx, Dollar Shave Club, and so on. Here no heavy investments are required.[71]

How to define failure in the **PISA case**? Let's recall that the previously suggested test indicated that more than *50 percent* of those surveyed were willing to buy the innovation. Because it has *competitive advantage* over the alternative (it gets the job done better). Potential clients *react* and feel *emotional* about the problem (as assessed by behavioral interviews and direct emotional assessment). Also a search concluded there is *no present solution* for the problem in the market. The *break-even level is low* (below 3 percent of market share of the most similar product). *Price was set covering all costs.* And the *ratio of price to cost is over* **2.5** *providing flexibility.*

These **eight reasons** ensure that market entry was carefully analyzed. So, there is no reason to expect profits and cash flow to be negative after the short period of **three years**. Which is a long enough period to allow, if need be, corrective **actions** in promotion channels, models, type of clients targeted, and so on.

That is a reasonable **definition of failure**: monthly negative profits **and** cashflow at the end of **three years**. Not accumulated[72] but the **latest**

And whatever the definition of failure the company opts for **at the end of X years**, it is always advantageous to establish **intermediate targets** of clients or sales, which indicate meanwhile whether one is on or off the correct path.

If off alerting for the need of immediate corrective action (**Disney ESPN** in the earlier example decreased the price, offered more customers incentives, and so on) and within a relatively short timeframe.

The assessment period for **Disney** was one year. And for **Amazon**—because it was even more off track—only six months. Other businesses tend to take a longer view of two, three, and even in some instances more years.

[71]Although all these companies are unicorns as per Figure 1 in Chapter 1.

[72]If accumulated would mean that the payback period was more than three years.

months at the end of the third year should be of constant profits and positive cash.

There is **one exception**: when profits are positive but cash negative. That is acceptable under three (**all necessary**) **conditions**:

First: it is *forecasted* with great probability that cash will become positive soon (within a few months);

Second: the forecasted date is far before all *cash reserves* will be exhausted (there is therefore a cushion);

Third: cash being negative at the end of the third year was *already predicted*, or the difference between forecast and reality is not greater than 25 percent (1/4)—see **Figure 24**.

Unless these **three** conditions are met, it does not seem reasonable to accept a negative cashflow at the end of three years: after all the tests performed on the project it nevertheless brings strong negative surprises. How come?

THE DEFINITION OF FAILURE FOR PISA'S INNOVATIONS			
R U L E	The months at the end of a 3-year period must be	1	**Profitable**
			and
		2	**Positive cashflow**
E X C E P T I O N S	Cash[1] negative but	A	There are reserves (the company is not about to be cash strapped)
			and
		B	Cashflow as forecasted (or difference not greater than **25%**)
			or
		C	Highly probable that cash will become positive soon
(1) – Always monthly profits, not losses.			

Figure 24

If three years down the road the project insists on negative outcomes**, it is not a project, it is a mistake** that should not be pursued any further.

If the horse is dead dismount. Letting it go, more than giving up is buoying up. Most specially since one is dealing with technically simple (PISA) projects (not music streaming businesses as Spotify, Napster, or Tidal).

And that were repeatedly pretested. *Why should one still be losing money after three years?*

5.7. Gradual Implementation

Traveler, there is no way one makes it as one moves along is a saying attributed to both the Spanish and Portuguese poets Antonio Machado and Fernando Pessoa.

Thus market entry should be **gradual**; step by step. Bringing **two advantages.**

5.7.1. The Advantages

First, since an entrepreneur faces unchartered territory, **mistakes** will occur. E. Musk's SpaceX failed multiple rocket launches, threatened bankruptcy until success. Oprah Winfrey was fired from her first TV job. Sara Blakely struggled until finding the right fabrics for Spanx, the shoeless pantyhoses. Richard Branson, the founder of Virgin group, launched a Virgin Cola that failed to gain any traction.

That failures and mistakes will occur is **not** an issue. The **question** is if one will learn from them, or one will be submerged by them. Will they be *teachers or undertakers?*

The distinction lies on the **rhythm** of the market entry.

Bolivar who achieved independence for South America said that it is in defeat that one learns how to win. Peter Drucker once asked Alfred Sloan, the CEO of General Motors, why he didn't fire a manager he was furious with because of a major blunder. "Are you crazy?, after the fortune that costed him to learn the lesson?", was the answer.

Shai Agassi

On the other hand, Shai Agassi, the Israeli entrepreneur that emulatled E. Musk with electric cars, was forced out of the market. For too much, too fast, geographic and product dispersion (e.g., not focusing on the Tokyo taxi market where he had an early great success).

Thus the first reason for *if in a hurry, go slow* is the need **to learn** as one moves along; to digest mistakes rather than being overcome by them.

Peter Drucker

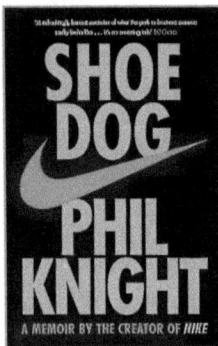

The second reason is **cash**: all new ventures, as Peter Drucker stressed, are cash strapped.

Sales may increase. And profits made. But cash is always scarce. Not only expansion requires immediate cash for new design, orders, personnel, and infrastructure, but also money is tied up in inventories, and in the difference between the terms of payments and receivables. On top of that the increase in value of trademarks, logos, and patents represents profits, but does not count for immediate cash.

As **Phil Knight** stresses in his memoirs, for years he would repeatedly, endlessly, have to calm down employees, banks, suppliers, and even his

49 percent co-shareholder Bowerman by saying: *we are not broke, we just don't have any money.*[73]

In other words: we have profits (and sales), but no cash. A small distinction, which makes a great difference.

Nike, between its inception in 1964 and when it went public in 1980, was always both a sales success and a highly profitable company, but always, always, *cash strapped.* And thus in the fringe of bankruptcy. Phil Knight would come home, tried to talk to his wife, and she would refuse, complaining: *here comes the wall.*

In 1975 were it not for the personal intervention of the management of the Japanese trading company Nissho, and Nike would have gone under.[74]

Elon Musk was also constantly running out of cash. He benefited however from clients paying beforehand, government help, and an adequate choice of models (first sports and then a car of the year sedan). A sedan was also the choice of Shai Agassi, but a wrong one, since the Israeli market demanded a subcompact.

Both entrepreneurs experienced extreme cash difficulties. Musk survived. Agassi did not. And in any case as Peter Drucker stressed: *in entrepreneurship **cash,** not profit, is king.*

---

[73]Knight, P. (2016). Shoe Dog: A Memoir by the Creator of Nike. Simon & Schuster..

[74]In an example of courage and loyalty, **Mr. Ito**, the top representative of Nissho in the United States, walked into Nike's major bank, which had cut all funding as well as denouncing Nike to the FBI, and paid all outstanding loans. Without any obligation to that, whatsoever. Only because he believed in the Nike project and had seen all accounting. That single handedly saved Nike.

In short, market entry should be **gradual** to **digest** rather than succumb to mistakes since **cash** will always be scarce.

But how to do it?

5.7.2. Entering the Market Gradually

That involves *first* of all a **single product** at start.[75]

Nike today makes all types of sports items. For men, women, and children. Garments (jackets and so on), apparel equipment (speed ropes, bottles, backpacks), and shoes alike. For all sorts of sports (running, basketball, tennis, soccer, football, golf, even skate) and also for everyday use. And all sorts of brands under the Nike umbrella.[76]

In the beginning *Nike* was called Blue Ribbon Sports.[77] The **single product** was sneakers and the **only model** the **Onitsuka Tiger** specialized for running, both on track (competition) and off track jogging. They

---

[75]Thus the focus when selecting among alternative innovations in Section 3.2 of Chapter 3.
[76]Some of the most popular include:

1. Nike SB (Skateboarding): tailored for skateboarders, often featuring extra durability and impact protection;
2. Nike Air Max series that have visible air cushioning in the sole: Nike Air Max 1, Air Max 90, Air Max 270, and Air Max 97;
3. Nike Air Force 1: a basketball shoe;
4. Nike Flyknit: shoes constructed using lightweight and breathable Flyknit material for comfort;
5. Nike Zoom series: running shoes such as Nike Zoom Pegasus, Zoom Vomero, and Zoom Structure;
6. Nike Free series: lightweight and flexible running shoes that mimic the sensation of running barefoot;
7. Nike Blazer: classic basketball shoes with a retro look;
8. Nike Air Jordan: basketball shoes created in collaboration with basketball player Michael Jordan;
9. Nike Cortez: a running shoe with a simple design.

[77]The official name of the company became Nike only in 1971.

were creamy white and with blue stripes down the sides. In Phil Knight's words: *God, they were beautiful.* An inventory of 12 pairs of shoes manufactured by the Japanese factory Onitsuka was enough to convince Bowerman (Phil Knight's former athletics coach) to join as a shareholder and for Nike to get started.

Jack Lalanne created the first fitness company that at the time of his death was offering health pre-prepared meals, a variety of foods in a chain of health stores, a TV program, books, specially designed exercising machines, and even kitchen items such as juicers.

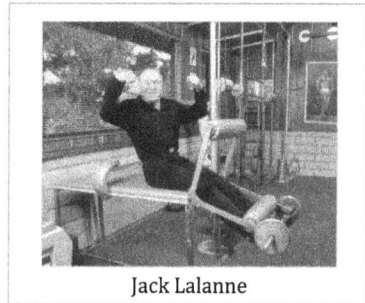

Jack Lalanne

But it started as and remained for long solely **specialized** in gymnasiums and in a **single** location: Oakland, California.

At later stages, after the early success, there is a powerful Peter Drucker question to drive business expansion: *what are the unsatisfied needs of our customer?*, which led Gerber to go from toys to baby lotions, to handkerchief bibs, to talcum powder, to shampoos, to nappies and food (see Figure 25).

But at the beginning, better a single product, as *men who chase two rabbits, catch neither* (Confucius).

Second, a **single model** for the first product.

Down the road, there is another very useful Peter Drucker question to set the expansion path: *what _other_ jobs can our product do?*

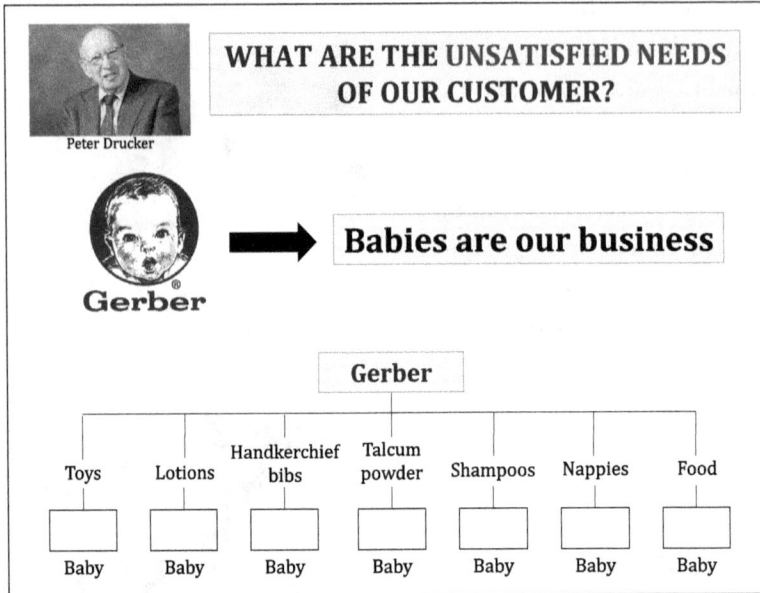

Figure 25

Febreze started as a surface cleaner and then moved into a product in search of other jobs to do, by adding new models for laundry additives, sprays to remove odors, air fresheners (candles, plugs, wax melts, for cars), pet odor eliminator, and so on. As a result Febreze is today the number one brand in the market.

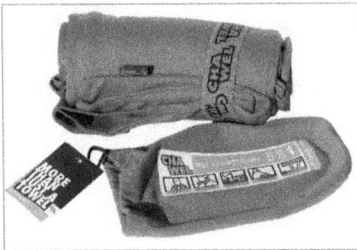

But in the beginning, there was only the surface cleaner model, just as *Chawel*[8] started with only the single model sportive (for beach, lake, and river) and only latter added the traveler model (for camping and mountaineering) and in-between

---

[8]The five in one for clothes changing, towel, sleeping bag, blanket, and pillow neck in airplanes.

the hybrid model and further differentiated between two sizes: average and big.

Then piecemeal market entry, also means at start focusing on **a single type of client** and *slowly trickling down*.

TRX (total body resistance system) initially using only parachutes strips for exercising was promoted and sold solely to Navy Seals, since the entrepreneur Randy Hetrick being a member of them knew the instructors best.

Then with time came the *trickle down to:*

- Other special military units such as rangers, delta forces, green berets;
- The marines;
- The U.S. military in general; and finally
- Three types of civilians: middle lower and lower social classes frequently on the road (salesmen, backpackers); youngsters unwilling to pay a gymnasium fee; and people living in isolated homes (**Figure 26**).

In **fourth** place, both *geography* and *time* should expand piece by piece.

Gorillas' business model of supermarket groceries delivered in 10 minutes came to be a unicorn present at its peak in over 60 cities of nine countries.[79]

But it started with **Kagan Sümer** delivering groceries only to his Berlin neighborhood, using his own bike, a mobile app, and goods bought from the local supermarket and then stored at his flat. Once an order came in, he hopped on his bike and delivered it (the Gorillas app was only available within his neighborhood to ensure deliveries on time).

---

[79]After its acquisition by Getir and as per January 2024: 19 cities in four countries, due to restructuring to maximize synergy between the two companies.

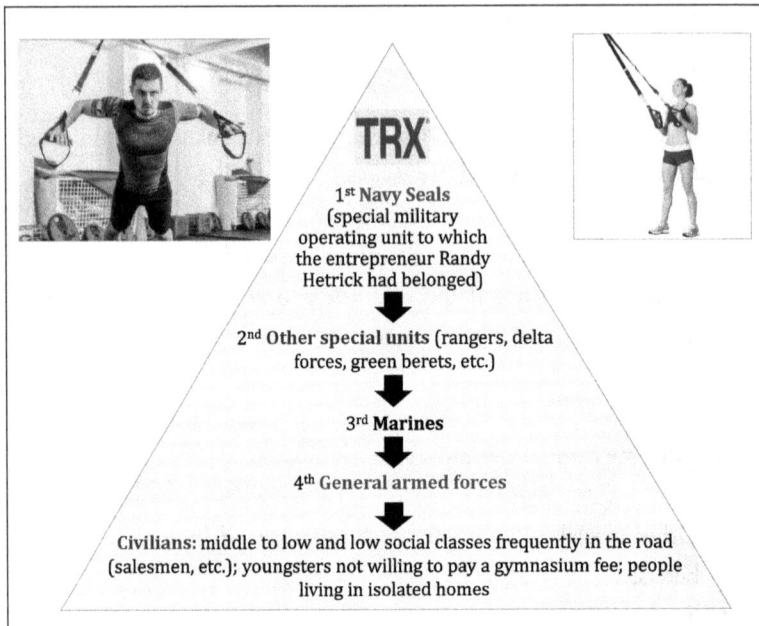

Figure 26 The TRX trickle down

After the first phase, Gorillas offer was expanded to customers in Prenzlauer Berg, a district of 165,000 people located in the center of Berlin. And so on.

Phil Knight, after being rejected by a couple of sporting goods stores (*kid, what this world does not need is another track shoe*) drove to various track meetings. Between races he would chat up the coaches, runners, and fans and show them the sneakers. But **only** in the Pacific Northwest around his Portland hometown in Oregon.

And *Jack Lalanne* after being successful with his first gym in Oakland expanded to other cities, but again **solely** in California.

Besides geography, **time** may also at first be limited and only later expanded.

Zuckerberg offered Facebook for free for 24 hours and it took fire. MooseX, the personal trainer service on demand, where the customer chooses the place and time, started by being offered only on Saturday mornings.

Fifth, specialization is also useful in **magazines, fairs and shows, stores, and online.**

Newman's Own, the salads and dressings company founded by **Paul Newman**, sparked its success with news placed on culinary magazines for housewives.

Bette Nesmith, the inventor of Liquid Paper (the white ink corrector), sent samples to magazines specialized in office products, such as The Office and The Secretary, which then wrote articles on the innovation, resulting in thousands of inquiries about the product.

Fairs and shows are also excellent venues. **Bette Nesmith** rented the most modest spaces, with a bare chair and a table to put on Liquid Paper. Within a few years it had sold 25 million product units for a $1.5 million in profits.

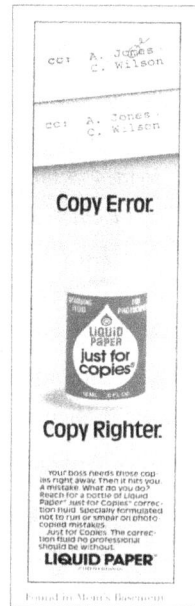

Ed Lowe, the innovator of granulated clay that acted as a sand substitute for cats' boxes, couldn't even afford any space in fairs. So, he offered to clean all cats' boxes in exchange for rent and his business took off.

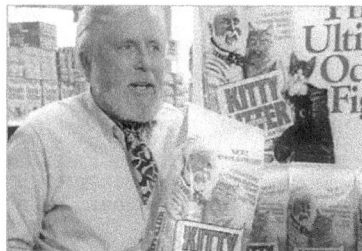

Sometimes specialized stores are harder to get into, so Ed Lowe left the product at consignation in pet shops, while **Art Fry** left the Post-its near the cashiers for customers to pick up for free at first. And then they never stopped coming back for more. But now … paying.

And here the internet is another way to progressively test market temperature (eBay, Etsy, Google Ads, and so on), both regarding if the product sells and what is its popularity (customer ratings).

Finally, gradually also means customers' orders **preceding** those to suppliers. The objective is to minimize inventory.

In Phil Knight's words, Nike was constantly at risk of bankruptcy because:

> *I was to blame. I refused to consider ordering less inventory. Why cut an order from 3 down to 2 million if I believed the demand out there is for 5 million? Thus I would order a number of shoes that seemed absurd and we'd need to stretch to pay for. To most observers this would've seemed a brazenly reckless, dangerous way of doing business, but I believed demand was greater than sales.*

So, unless the product cost (but not the price) is very low, such as with Post-its, Liquid Paper, and Kitty Litter, the bankruptcy risk increases sharply if clients' orders do not precede those of suppliers, with a minimum inventory in-between.

Figure 27 summarizes the essentials of gradual implementation.

At the start one establishes **two squares** for focus. **The narrower, the better.**

The sides of the **larger square** are *product* (one), *model* (one), *client* type (one), and *geography* (narrow).

And of the **smaller square** are limited *time* offer, specialized *promotion* channels (fairs and events, magazines and internet sites), specialized *delivery* channels (stores), and finally customers' orders *preceding* those to suppliers.

Then one expands. Progressively by letting go an increasing numbers of sides of both squares.

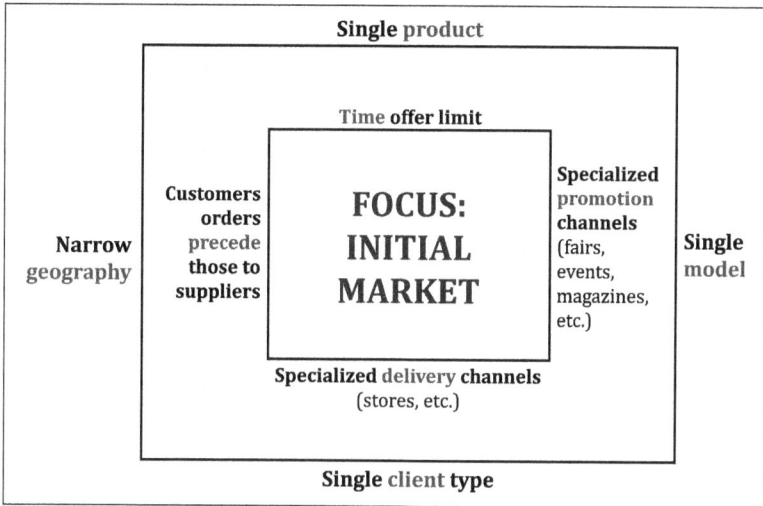

Figure 27 Gradual market entry: By releasing an increasing number of square sides

5.8. Concluding

The <u>A</u> of PISA, **Action, starts** with building a **prototype**. What a seven-year-old like Cassidy Crowley (of Baby Toon) can do. And a single one or a few for promotional offers (Nike started with 12 pairs of shoes made in the Japanese factory Onitsuka).

A **provisional (low cost) patent** provides protection during one year. **Names** and **logos** are best to be trademarked too. The story of Margaret Knight illustrates that all are a must. **And Sara Blakely of the unicorn Spanx** exemplifies that they all can be made by the entrepreneur single-handedly.

Then the adequate **price level** is set and **four tests** performed on the innovation: *price-to-cost ratio* hopefully high to provide flexibility regarding unforeseen events (and above the economy average of *2.5*).

A *low break-even* is required (below the *3 percent* market share). Next, does the innovation get the job better done (and so has *competitive advantage* over the alternatives including doing nothing)? And finally in an **anonymous survey** (in Momentive/SurveyMonkey or other online sites) more than *50 percent* of the respondents are definitely going to buy the product.

The time for **market entry** has then come. Accompanied with a **focus group** (to coach on improvements and new models), a **clear definition of failure** so that the new venture is a new beginning, not a life's ruin (monthly positive profits and cashflow at the end of three years), and **gradually** (Figure 27 before).

After all the above, can one be **100 percent sure** of success?

No, because as Nike's Phil Knight recognizes, **luck** plays a big role. *Call it Tao, Jnana or Dharma or Baraka (a north African term, may we add).*

But the harder you work, the better your Tao.

Winston Churchill

In the present case, **hard work** means **due preparation**, leaving no loose ends and creating assurance: that **everything was done for success.**

The only certainty, because of Baraka, is not of success but because of preparation that we merit it.

Winston Churchill put it best: *we cannot be certain of victory; only that we deserve it.*

CHAPTER 6

Conclusion: The Way Forward

To change is to improve; to change often is perfection.

If we keep on doing what worked in the past, we are going to fail.

Winston Churchill

Peter Drucker

Entrepreneurship is a glamorous field. However, **five** issues that were **true** in the **past** are today **myths**.

First innovations have been associated with highly **sophisticated products**.

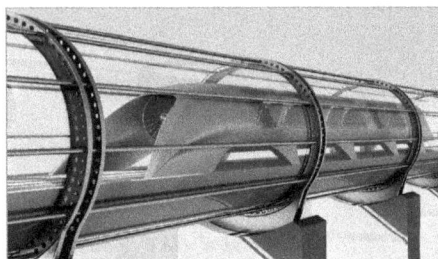

Elon Musk revolutionized *four* industries: *payments* (with PayPal), *satellites* for information and communications (SpaceX), *energy* (SolarCity), and *transportation* (Tesla), leaving aside the most recent Boring, the high-speed trains still in the project phase.[80]

Apple structurally redefined *three* other industries: *information technology* (with PCs), *telecommunications* (smartphones), and *music* (iPod, iTunes).

And then of course there are eBay, Microsoft, Amazon, Dell, YouTube, Google, the streaming companies of videos (Netflix), music (Spotify), or graphic design (Canva) and so on.

However, the glamour of those technically sophisticated innovations overshadows a second part of reality: the dozens and dozens of **unicorns** that are **simple**. Not technologically complex, requiring high know-how and large investment in R&D.

A few examples of such unicorns are Spanx, Rent the Runway, Dollar Shave Club, Gorillas, Warby Parker,

---

[80]Twitter (now X) was a E. Musk takeover, not an innovation.

Gymshark, Fenty Beauty, Harry's, Gousto, Vestiaire Collective, Athletic Greens, and Havaianas.

And then of course there are those that have not yet achieved unicorn status but are nevertheless worth in the multitude of millions: Knix, Drop Stop, Pouchee, Lisa Gable Accessories, Readerest, SafeGrabs, or Chawel.

Their impact on daily life is measured by their *value*. *Nike* is a $170 billion company started by Phil Knight ordering from the Japanese factory Onitsuka 12 pairs of shoes, that had a fancy design, were cheaper and specialized for racing, and thus slightly different from those manufactured by the giants that then dominated the industry: Adidas, Puma, Reebok, and Converse.

In the past there was no justification for simple innovations to be of high worth. **But modern life is complex**. Thus nowadays anything that brings simplicity is much valued. Because as Constantin Brancusi put it: **simplicity is complexity solved.**

And so at present, on the one hand **accumulated knowledge** enables an increasing number of sophisticated innovations. And on the other, **complexity** opens the door to start-ups that contribute to **simplicity**.

A **second** myth is that to find opportunities one must invest at least considerable **time** actively **searching** for them.

However, many great ideas just **came** directly toward the entrepreneur, that is, met she or he as they would go about their daily activities. And they came in the form of **problems** (to be solved) of one of **five** types.

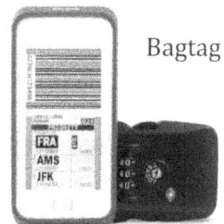

Bagtag

Bothers: SockTabs, Funk-tional, BagTag, Fog-Block, TwistieMag, among other examples previously analyzed.

Soundbender

Incompetent products: Elevators, Drop Stop, the Ice Cream Canteen (worth millions), The Sleep Styler, Soundbender, Sheertex, or Go Pro (IPO of $4 billion in 2014).

Removing complications: Day2Night, Tanya Heath, Pouchee, Ninu, Comfy, SafeGrabs, Chawel, Doppelganger.

Worries, concerns: Baby Toon, Lisa Gable strap, Grayl, Objemer, Eyelights, Bumpsters, Safetytat, or Athletic Greens.

And bringing moments of *true happiness* to merely "content" daily lives: Vestiaire Collective, Miss O & Friends, GymShark, Gousto, or Nissin Foods (the precooked instant noodles requiring only pouring hot water).

Vestiaire Collective

All the above examples are worth millions, frequently in the hundreds, sometimes **unicorns**.

Third, there is the myth that a solution requires **considerable effort to build**.

In fact, many valuable innovations are simply imports from elsewhere with no changes at all, or only small adaptations of products. They are serving other needs, clients, geographies, or distribution channels.

As illustrated in Chapter 4 by Athelas, Fresh Paper, Too Good To Go, Havaianas, TernX Carry On, L'eggs, Fenty Beauty, TRX, Lola Rola, or the StashAll line of bags.

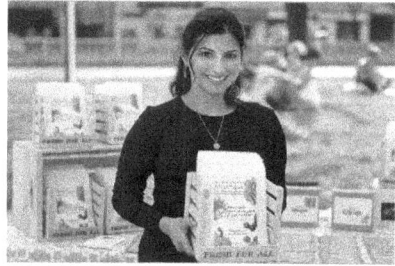

Fresh Paper

Kitty Litter, the granulated clay used in construction, became a company worth $400 million when applied as a substitute of sand to cat litter boxes.

Other examples are the American icons Barbie, the American Girl doll, and the hub systems first introduced into the United States by Delta Airlines and Federal Express, but copied from the Indian Post Office.

A **fourth anachronism** respects how **to test** innovations before market entry.

Today we know that asking customers about their interest is an unreliable predictor of behavior: Colgate, McDonald's, Evian, Harley Davidson, Pepsico, Microsoft, or Apple, to name a few demonstrate that.

People do not *act* as they *say*, do not *say* what they *think*, do not *think* what they *feel*, but *act* as they **feel**.[81]

Thus, rather than *words* and *thoughts* far better to tap into **actions** and **emotions**. And there is for such a purpose *two nonexpensive tests (behavioral interviews and direct emotional assessment)* that are a consequence of the **prospect theory revolution**, which in the last two decades produced **two Nobel Prizes** (D. Kahneman and R. Thaler).

---

[81]First said by the marketeer David Ogilvy.

Finally (and as a consequence of the above) there is a **fifth belief** that no longer holds true: that entrepreneurs in order to be successful have to be **highly educated**, or at least **experts** in some area. Or even of a certain **age**.

Abbey Fleck

Companies worth **millions** were created by: Cassidy Crowley (7 years old), Abbey Fleck (8 years), Lilly Hooks (9 years), Richie Stachowski (10 years), Cassidy Goldstein (12 years), Kavita Shukla (13 years), Sarah Buckel (14 years), and Catherine Cook (15 years).

Sarah Buckel

On the other hand: John Cover Jr., when creating Taser was 50 years old, Anita Crook of Pouchee (59 years), Wally Blume of Denali (the ice cream and cookies company, 60 years), Mary Tennyson of Stash-All (63 years), Lisa Gable of L.G. Accessories (70 years), and Doris Drucker, the wife of the great professor of management, Peter Drucker, was 82 years old when she introduced Visivox.

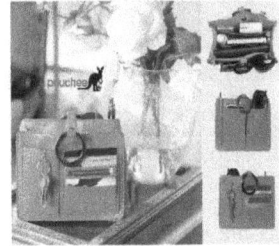

Doris Drucker

Age? *Simply a number.*

Along the book other common beliefs were questioned (e.g., as in Section 5.6 of Chapter 5) that **perseverance means never giving up**. *Phil Knight of Nike* denounces as charlatans those who defend that and *Einstein defined madness as keeping on doing the same things and expect different results.*

Reconciliation of perseverance with the decision of giving up is done by **change**: of product *models*; *client* types; *geography*; *time*; channels of *promotion*; or *distribution*. In *Peter Drucker's* words: changing gears, together with a clear definition of failure.

Another myth is that the **import of innovations** works only if from richer to **poorer countries**. Indeed it works both ways as Section 4.2 in Chapter 4 exemplified with major innovations the United States imported from India.

And there is no reason to question the **social value** of simple innovations. Even the simplest ones (such as SockTabs and TwistieMag) save the scarcest of all resources: **time**. A resource that every single day comes closer and closer to extinction.

Simple innovations can even be **life savers**. Drop Stop, the seat gap filler, was invented by Newburguer after he almost killed both a side walker and himself, while driving and at the same time trying to grab a phone that had fallen to the floor of his car.

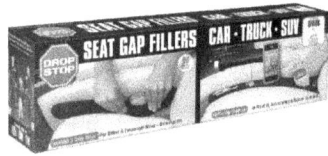

Thus, where do all the above leave us? **What is this book's message?**

It brings a **simple method (PISA)** to create **highly valuable innovations** as people go about their **daily lives** of work, family, and leisure. Without requiring any change in habits.

Also it stresses that *for innovation to have social benefits, it does not have to be social innovation.* That is, done by nonprofit organizations.

SHE that produces sanitary pads is a company founded by Elizabeth Scharpf, who when working for the World Bank in Mozambique discovered that many women would periodically miss school and work because they could not afford sanitary pads.

SUSTAINABLE
HEALTH
ENTERPRISES

Instead of the traditional, short-term and nonsustainable solution of charity, **E. Scharpf** created a long-term, sustainable one, by acting on price.

After testing different fibers abundant in Africa, she concluded that the best absorbent material was made of banana. Most abundant in **Rwanda**.

So a factory there created **600** jobs serving the market of Mozambique and other African countries and thus solving a **social problem**. And the outcome is a very profitable private company.

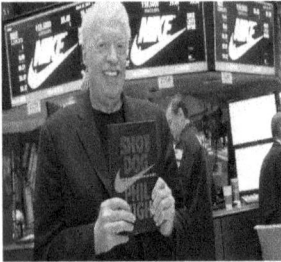

Phil Knight

Any type of successful innovation is social as it contributes to progress. In **Phil Knight's** words: *When one makes or improves something one makes the lives of strangers happier, healthier, or safer, or better, one is participating fully in the whole grand human drama. More than simply alive, one helps others to live more fully.*

And that requires neither **money**, nor **instruction**, **age,** or **country**. But simply an **attitude**: not being happy with the way things are and wanting to be part of progress. To wish to make a difference, a dent in the universe.

B. Shaw

In the words of **Bernard Shaw**, *reasonable people **adapt** themselves to the world; **unreasonable** people **try to adapt** the world to them; thus all **progress** depends on the **latter**.*

It is to them that this book is dedicated.

Bibliography

Becraft, M. B. 2014. *Bill Gates: A Biography*. Greenwood.

Drucker, P. F. 2007. *Innovation and Entrepreneurship*. Elsevier.

DuDell, M. P. 2013. *Shark Tank Jump Start Your Business: How to Launch and Grow a Business from Concept to Cash*. Kingswell.

Forbes Inc. 1997. *Forbes? Great Minds of Business*, edited by G. Morganson. John Wiley & Sons

Isaacson, W. 2011. *Steve Jobs*. Simon & Schuster.

Isaacson, W. 2023. *Elon Musk*. Simon & Schuster.

Kirkpatrick, D. 2010. *The Facebook Effect: The Inside Story of the Company That Is Connecting the World*. Simon & Schuster.

Knight, P. 2016. *Shoe Dog: A Memoir by the Creator of Nike*. Simon & Schuster.

Kotler, P. 2017. *My Adventures in Marketing: The Autobiography of Philip Kotler*. Idea Bite Press.

Litwicki, E. 2000. "Tupperware: The Promise of Plastic in 1950s America." *Journal of Social History* 34: 247–249.

Magretta, J. 1998. "The Power of Virtual Integration: An Interview with Dell Computer's Michael Dell." *Harvard Business Review*, March–April. https://hbr.org/1998/03/the-power-of-virtual-integration-an-interview-with-dell-computers-michael-dell.

Mancuso, J. 1982. *Have You Got What It Takes?: How to Tell If You Should Start Your Own Business*. Prentice-Hall.

Maslow, A. H. 1943. "A Theory of Human Motivation." *Psychological Review* 50 (4): 370–396.

Monaghan, T., and R. Anderson. 1986. *Pizza Tiger*. Random House.

Ogilvy, D. 1987. *Confessions of an Advertising Man*. Pan Books.

O'Grady, J. D. 2009. *Apple Inc*. Greenwood Press.

Oliver, T. 1986. *The Real Coke, the Real Story*. Random House.

Omidyar, P. 2011. "How I Did It: EBay's Founder on Innovating the Business Model of Social Change." *Harvard Business Review*, September. https://hbr.org/2011/09/ebays-founder-on-innovating-the-business-model-of-social-change.

Schlender, B., and R. Tetzeli. 2015. *Becoming Steve Jobs: The Evolution of a Reckless Upstart into a Visionary Leader*. Crown Business.

Schwartz, B. 2004. *The Paradox of Choice: Why More Is Less*. Ecco.

Smith, D. 2013. *How to Think Like Steve Jobs*. Michael O'Mara Books Limited.

Strauss, S. D. 2002. *The Big Idea: How Business Innovators Get Great Ideas to Market*. Dearborn Trade Publishing.

Ulwick, A. W. 2016. *Jobs to Be Done, Theory to Practice*. Idea Bite Press.

Vance, A. 2015. *Elon Musk—How the Billionaire CEO of SpaceX and Tesla Is Shaping Our Future*. Penguin Random House.

About the Authors

JORGE SÁ

1. Jorge Sá is an expert on Peter Drucker and Philip Kotler, founders of modern management and modern marketing, respectively, with whom he studied and who offered letters of recommendation for his books and endorsements for his work.

2. He has a **master's degree** from the Peter F. Drucker Graduate School of Management in California and a **doctorate (PhD)** in Business Administration, from Columbia University, in New York, where he was a research, teaching assistant, and graduated with honors (always Dean's list, Beta Gamma Sigma). He also holds *two undergraduate degrees* (in business administration and economics) and a *graduate degree* in macroeconomics.

3. He was awarded the **Jean Monnet Chair** by the Jean Monnet Foundation in **Brussels**, and his **books translated into 12 languages: English, Portuguese, Spanish, Chinese (Mandarin), Russian, Ukrainian, German, Lithuanian, Thai, Korean, Norwegian, and Iranian**; he received **endorsements**, among others, from Peter F. Drucker, Cecily Drucker, Al Ries (author of the bestsellers *Marketing Warfare* and *Positioning*), Don Hambrick (professor at Columbia University and The Pennsylvania State University), Karl Moore (professor at Oxford and McGill University), Peter Starbuck (president of the London Drucker Society), and Philip Kotler.

4. Besides **over 40 articles published in blind refereed** academic reviews and journals (Scopus) of economics, business administration,

and medicine, he has addressed **conferences and given seminars** at several institutions including TED USA (https://youtu.be/SOk-jPVi1Fts), London Business School, Drucker University, IESE, Glasgow Business School, ESSEC (France), ESSAM (European Consortium of Business Schools), Manchester Business School, George Washington University, Oxford, and so on. He has also addressed conferences and presented articles in academic and non-academic meetings, such as the Academy of Management, Western Economic Association, Peter Drucker Society of Europe, the European Commission, and so on.

5. He has worked as a **private consultant, non-executive director** or taught in the **executive programs** of *multinational companies* such as: Coca-Cola, SHELL, Unisys, IBM, Price Waterhouse, KPMG, Glaxo, British Petroleum—BP, Dun & Bradstreet, Deloitte & Touche, Makro (Metro group), Systéme U, I.F.A, Intermarché, Mini Prix Bonjours, Accenture, Watson Wyatt, Cap Gemini, Cesce, Scottish & Newcastle, Sara Lee, Total, Johnson & Johnson, Pfizer, Logica, Indra, Grandvision, Jafep, Euler Hermes, Cosec, Pestana Group Hotels, Tivoli Hotels & Resorts, Millennium Bank, Julius Baer, SGG, Henkel, Abencys, Broadbill, Volkswagen Group, McDonald's, MiTek, United Steel Products, Base Group, UnitedHealth group, Inapa, Vodafone, IDC, Merck, BPI Bank, Milestone, Fijowave, Foxpak, ND Sports, LLR-G5, Horan, Prodieco, Dennison, Grid Finance, Bluemetrix, European Federation of Pharmaceutical Industries and Associations, Microsoft, and so on.

6. His **hobbies** are *history* (wrote several books on the lessons of military campaigns for management) and *football/soccer* (degree as a professional coach). He speaks and writes (by alphabetical order) English, French, German, Portuguese, and Spanish. He lives between Lisbon and Rio de Janeiro. And the office, Vasconcellos e Sá Associates (www.vasconcellosesa.com), provides support for research and other activities.

MAGDA PEREIRA

Has an undergraduate degree in Management by ISEG School of Economics & Management.

Magda Pereira is the general manager at Vasconcellos e Sá Associates.

She wrote books in coauthorship with Professor Jorge Sá and managed many consultancy projects for Vasconcellos e Sá Associates.

NADIIA NIKITINA

Has a master's degree in chemistry by Vasyl' Stus Donetsk National University and an undergraduate degree in ecology by the Volodymyr Dahl East Ukrainian National University.

Nadiia Nikitina is a director at Vasconcellos e Sá Associates and wrote books in coauthorship with Professor Jorge Sá.

Index

.

www.ingramcontent.com/pod-product-compliance
Lightning Source LLC
Chambersburg PA
CBHW061310220326
41599CB00026B/4824